CHICKENS
IN YOUR
BACKYARD

A Beginner's Guide

CHICKENS
IN YOUR
BACKYARD

A Beginner's Guide

NEWLY REVISED AND UPDATED

GAIL DAMEROW
AND RICK LUTTMANN

RODALE.

Published in the United States by Rodale Books,
an imprint of the Crown Publishing Group, a division of
Penguin Random House LLC, New York.

crownpublishing.com
rodalebooks.com

RODALE and the Plant colophon are registered trademarks of
Penguin Random House LLC.

Originally published in different form by Rodale Books, an imprint of
the Crown Publishing Group, a division of Penguin Random House LLC in 1976.

Library of Congress Cataloging-in-Publication Data is available upon request.

ISBN 978-1-63565-096-9
Ebook ISBN 978-1-63565-097-6

Book design by Joanna Williams
Illustrations by Sidney Quinn
Illustrations on pages 7, 26, 27, 36, 37, 39, 75, 79, and 121 by Bethany Caskey
Cover design by Christina Gaugler
Cover illustrations by Sidney Quinn

Revised Edition

147506545

IN MEMORY OF GEORGE MATSON, WHO OFFERED ENCOURAGEMENT WHEN WE WROTE THE FIRST EDITION OF THIS BOOK, WHO ALWAYS KNEW HOW TO MAKE US LAUGH, AND WHO CONTINUES TO LIVE IN OUR HEARTS

CONTENTS

CONTENTS

CHICKENS
IN YOUR
BACKYARD

A Beginner's Guide

INTRODUCTION: BEFORE THE BEGINNING

Is it any wonder that no one can decide which came first, the chicken or the egg? Raising chickens is a continuous cyclical process, and the only way to describe it is to break into the cycle at an arbitrary point and call it the beginning. In organizing this book, we've chosen one place to start, but your immediate needs may require you to skip chapters of no urgency to you at the moment.

You really should have your facilities and feed lined up before acquiring your first chickens, but if you want to dream about your future flock while making preparations for their arrival, you might want to skip to Starting Your Flock on page 135. We've tried to organize the information presented here to make it easy for you to jump around as much as you like and to skip chapters that you don't immediately need; you may not be ready to hatch eggs in an incubator, for instance, and you may never be ready to harvest homegrown chicken barbecue. We recommend, though, that you do read Chapter 1 first, so you will be up to speed on the meanings of specialized poultry-keeping terms.

In raising chickens ourselves and in talking about it with others, we've developed the philosophy that mindlessly following somebody else's list of rules is no substitute for a thorough understanding of the nature of chickens, the function of the equipment, and the purpose of the chicken keeper's various activities. For one thing, a little initiative can save you a lot of money. No need to buy the latest expensive chicken-keeping doodads when, with a little savvy, you might modify something you have lying around the garage to suit your needs. (If you can cleverly improvise even once, you may save far more than you spent on this book.) As long as your chickens' basic needs are met, there's no one right way of doing things, but there are plenty of wrong ways.

For another thing, people have such a variety of reasons for raising chickens that we have to allow for flexibility. Maybe you want a couple of pet bantams roaming in the backyard, or maybe you want your flock to supply eggs or meat for your family, or maybe you are mainly interested in winning first prize at the county fair. Your particular purpose will determine your perspective.

Finally, the better informed you are, the less likely you are to be an unhappy first-time chicken-keeper. For instance, we've frequently heard complaints from newbies whose hens aren't laying. Maybe the chickens are just reaching maturity and haven't yet started laying. Or, if it's winter, hens typically don't lay well (as you'll soon find out)–but by mid-spring, you'll be so sick of omelets, quiches, and Denver sandwiches that you'll be begging the hens to stop!

Of course, if you're truly unhappy with your chickens, it may be possible that you were the recipient of a "bad egg" or two. As in every industry, there are always a few who take deliberate advantage of the unwary, while some dealers may be merely incompetent or innocently ignorant. But most chicken-keepers are honest and helpful folks who are eager to share their experiences and their love of birds with you.

People who are just beginning to raise chickens occasionally express the opinion that all the lavish care chicken-raisers expend on their flocks seems unnatural and unnecessary, for surely chickens must have gotten along all right for thousands of years out there in the wild all by themselves. But, remember that chickens as we know them today have come a long way from their natural state, due to domestication and controlled breeding to suit our needs. The human race has made a Faustian bargain with chickens, and we must now pay the price of having molded them to our needs by giving them the care they have come to depend on, require, and deserve.

This book is a guide to enlightened intervention in the affairs of chickens.

It is intended for beginners–the ABC of keeping chickens, so to speak. When we wrote the first edition, we were experts in beginners' mistakes, having made most of them ourselves. We wrote the book after having looked everywhere for a good, clear, comprehensive, nontechnical, nonindustrial book about raising a flock in the backyard. It didn't exist. So, we wrote it.

Much has happened since then. The 21st-century chicken boom has brought a lot of new folks into the fold. The exponential increase in interest has been accompanied by innumerable new studies about the nature of chickens and their needs. The internet has spawned countless poultry-keeping blogs and forums, some offering sound advice, others spouting not-so-sound nonsense. With several more decades of chicken-keeping under our belts, our own knowledge has expanded. It's high time for an updated edition of this book. And here it is.

WORDS YOU SHOULD KNOW

A number of words are peculiar to the language of poultry-raising. Knowing and understanding these words will help you communicate with other people about chickens, especially when a word possesses a different or more precise meaning than it has in common usage. This chapter is intended as a reference both when unfamiliar words come up in your conversations with other poultry people and when these words occur in later chapters. This chapter serves as something of a glossary, with explanations developed more fully later on.

A bunch of chickens is officially called a *flock*. *Chicken* means a specific kind of bird, but it does not tell you the bird's sex. An adult female chicken is a *hen*, and an adult male is a *cock* or a *rooster*. Some folks just shorten it to *roo*.

A male chicken younger than 1 year is a *cockerel*, and a female chicken under 1 year is a *pullet*. (Don't confuse this word with *poult*, which is a baby turkey and has nothing to do with this book). A baby chicken of either sex is a *chick*. The sound a chick makes is a *peep*, and you'll sometimes see "peep" applied to the chick itself.

Chickens venture forth during the daytime, but they always return to the same place to sleep at night. This habit is called *roosting*, and the place they return to is the *roost*. Chickens like to sleep on something off the ground, like a tree branch or a ladder rung, which is referred to as a *perch*. Anytime a bird is sitting on such a thing, whether it is sleeping or not, it is *perching*.

Chickens come in two basic sizes: large and *bantam* (affectionately called *banty*). Bantams are not a separate breed or species; they are simply small

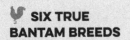
SIX TRUE BANTAM BREEDS

Dutch

Japanese

Nankin

Rosecomb

Sebright*

Serama*

*Gail's top picks

chickens. Some bantams have large counterparts; others do not. Those that do not are *true bantams*. Those that do are *miniatures*, although they are not exact miniatures–the size of their heads, tails, wings, feathers, and eggs is larger than would be the case if they were perfect miniatures.

Chickens, like horses and dogs, come in different breeds. *Purebreds* are those of one single breed sharing distinguishing characteristics that make them all alike. Since no organization registers chickens, purists take exception to the use of the word "purebred," preferring *straightbred*.

Hybrid-crosses, or *crossbreeds*, are developed for certain outstanding characteristics and are produced by always mating chickens of the same two different breeds. A chicken of mixed breed, often of unknown ancestry–a mutt of the chicken world–is a *barnyard chicken* or *barny*. To confuse the issue, however, when "barny" is capitalized, it refers to a specific breed, the Barnevelder.

Chickens that are purebred will breed true, which means that the offspring of a pair of chickens of the same breed will also be of the same breed and will, more or less, have the same characteristics. Barnies of indeterminate origin, and to a limited extent deliberately developed hybrids and crossbreeds, will have offspring with wild conglomerations of characteristics that can rarely be predicted accurately (but can be quite spectacular).

Pure breeds are grouped into different *classifications*, which usually tell the place of origin. Some classifications are Asiatic, American, and Mediterranean. Rhode Island Red is one of the breeds within the American classification, for example, and Leghorn is a breed within the Mediterranean classification. Breeds themselves are further organized into *varieties*, which tell more about the chickens' appearances. Brown Leghorn and white Leghorn are two varieties of the Leghorn breed. (Incidentally, Leghorn is pronounced LEG-ern, not LEG-horn.)

The *Standard*, with a capital *S*, refers to either of two books that describe the appearance of each breed and variety–color, weight, shape, feathering, and so forth. Both large and bantam breeds are described in the *American*

Standard of Perfection, a periodically updated book published by the American Poultry Association, and bantam breeds are additionally described in the *Bantam Standard,* published by the American Bantam Association. If you show your chickens, the extent to which they conform to their breed's standard description determines the prizes that they are awarded.

A *standard* or *standard-bred* chicken is any one described in either of these two books. The word "standard" is sometimes used incorrectly to refer to large-size chickens, as opposed to bantams.

The polite word for chicken excrement is *droppings,* also known as *chicken poop.* The polite word for the opening it comes out of is the *vent,* which also happens to be the same opening eggs come out of. Some of our friends find this fact appalling. (We refer them to the Manufacturer.) The eggs come along a different track, however, known as the *oviduct.* Just in front of the vent on the underside of the chicken are two sharp, pointed pubic bones coming back from the breastbone. By checking the distance between the pubic bones, you can tell how well a hen is laying.

Chickens don't have teeth. Whatever a chicken eats goes into a little pouch at the base of its neck called a *crop,* which usually bulges by the end of the day. The crop's contents are gradually released into the *gizzard,* which is essentially a sack of gravel and other small, hard objects that grind up everything to make it easier to digest. The grinding agent is called *grit.* If your chickens can't find grit naturally, in the form of sand or small pebbles pecked from your yard, you can purchase gravel grit at the feed store. (We are occasionally asked if chicken grit is the same product as grits sold at the grocery store. It isn't.)

Along with other types of chicken rations sold at a feed store is *scratch,* which consists of a mixture of corn and various grains. Scratch is not a nutritionally complete chicken feed. Think of it as candy for your feathered friends.

The part of a chicken's leg from the foot to the first joint is the *shank.* It is usually naked and scaly, but in some breeds, feathers grow all the way to the ground. *Spurs* are the sharp, horny protrusions on a cock's shank, which he uses to protect himself when he feels threatened. Their length and condition give you a rough idea of the cock's age. Hens sometimes grow spurs, but they're rarely as formidable as a rooster's. The superstructure on a chicken's head is a *comb,* and the dangly things under the chin are *wattles.*

The words "mate" and "breed" are not quite synonymous. *Mating* refers to

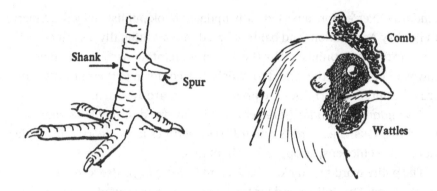

the forming of an allegiance between a male and a female, or sometimes a male and several females. Mated birds hang around together and have more social interaction with each other than with the rest of the flock. Wild birds tend to form strong matings, sometimes seasonal, sometimes for life. Chickens exhibit this behavior only mildly, in that a rooster usually tries to gather a harem of hens to supervise.

Breeding refers specifically to the performance of the sexual act. This word is also used in another sense–to refer to the genetic control exercised by a keeper to ensure that offspring are produced only by certain selective pairs of birds. Confusing these two meanings of the word can be rude, especially when you are talking to a chicken breeder.

The chickens you own are sometimes called your *stock*. If you save certain chickens specifically for breeding, they are called your *breeding stock* or your *breeders*. If you have excellent specimens of chickens suitable for exhibition, they are called *show stock* or *show quality* (abbreviated SQ). Those not of show quality (NSQ) are *pet quality* (PQ).

Serious breeders, and those who keep hens for economical egg production, periodically examine their chickens and remove any that are unhealthy, unproductive, or otherwise undesirable for their purposes. This process is called *culling*. For those who choose not to pass their problem chickens along to other chicken-keepers, cull means kill. For people who think of their chickens as beloved pets, cull is a four-letter word not to be mentioned in polite company.

An egg is described as *fertile* or *infertile* according to whether or not it is capable of producing a chick. Fertility depends on how recently a rooster has bred the hen that laid the egg and how vigorous the rooster is. When an egg is laid, it has a slimy wet covering, called the *bloom* or *cuticle*, that quickly dries and protects the egg's contents. A batch of eggs in a nest is called a *clutch*.

Eggs will hatch only if they are fertile, and they undergo a 21-day period of *incubation*, during which they must be kept suitably warm and moist. In nature, a hen accomplishes incubation by providing warmth and moisture from her body. This kind of sitting is called *setting*. Calvin Coolidge once remarked that, in his native rural Vermont, whether a hen was sitting or setting wasn't nearly as important as whether she was laying or lying.

A hen in the mood to set is said to be *broody.* If you don't want a hen to set, you have to *break her up*, which means discouraging her broodiness through various means. Some people call it *busting up*, because they think that sounds tougher, but hens are not so easily intimidated. You needn't worry that if you break up a hen that her deepest primal urgings will go unconsummated. She'll forget all about it in a day or two.

Assuming you elect not to break her up, or she elects to ignore your attempts, one day, a batch of chicks will *hatch* (chicks are never born). They make a hole in the eggshell through which they breathe while struggling to get out. The hole is called a *pip*, and making the hole is called *pipping.* The resulting batch of chicks is referred to as the hen's *brood*.

Incubation may be accomplished artificially in an *incubator,* or, by chicken-keepers who don't like long words, a *bator.* The device may be large or small, simple or elaborate, but it must imitate the temperature and humidity underneath a setting hen.

During incubation, you may want to see what's going on inside an egg by shining a light through it. This activity is called *candling,* even though it's no longer done with a candle. The same process, known by the same name, is also used to examine eggs for cracked shells or internal blood spots, when the eggs are sold for eating.

It's nice to know a baby chick's sex as soon as possible after it hatches. The process of sorting the pullets from the cockerels is called *sexing* and is done by professional *sexers* employed by a *hatchery*–a place that specializes in hatching chicks. When you buy chicks, you can get all pullets (for more money) or all cockerels (for less money)–but don't expect perfection, as even expert sexers are only about 95 percent accurate. You can also buy *straight-run* or *as-hatched* chicks, which means they have not been examined and sorted by sex, and they are mixed in natural proportions of about 50-50 (unless you are unlucky enough to get one of those all-too-frequent hatches that turn out to be 60 percent or more cockerels).

Chicks that are hatched without a hen are usually (but not necessarily) raised without a hen. While they are growing up, they must be kept warm and safe in an enclosure called a *brooder*.

At the time they hatch, chicks are covered with soft downy fluff rather than feathers. They begin to grow feathers immediately, however, and after they have a complete set of actual feathers, they are said to be *feathered-out*. Now they can fly and keep themselves warm, but they haven't yet acquired their full set of adult plumage. *Plumage* refers generally to a bird's configuration of feathers in all their different lengths, shapes, and colors. Once a year, usually in autumn, the feathers fall out and regrow. This occurrence is called the *molt*. Fortunately, the process occurs gradually, so a bird is seldom completely naked, though we've seen some come close.

Chicks sometimes *pick* each other, pulling out each other's feathers at the back, head, or vent. Older birds will also pick if too many are kept in too small a space, they get too hot, or they are simply bored. Sometimes, picking goes on so extensively that it turns into cannibalism. Shockingly, chickens will devour each other, if they have a mind to. They may also discover that eggs are good to eat. Then you have an *egg-eating* problem on your hands, which can be difficult to reverse.

A chicken yard is called a *pen* or a *run*, and the building where they lay their eggs and sleep is called a *coop*. Another common term is *henhouse*, which originated in the days when farmers kept a rooster only long enough to produce spring chicks for the next year's flock, then served him up for Sunday dinner. For most of the year, the chicken coop housed hens only; hence, henhouse.

Coop floors and brooder floors should be strewn with an absorbent material that is durable, does not pack easily, and permits quick evaporation of moisture from chicken droppings. Such material is called *litter* and commonly consists of pine shavings or shredded paper. If the litter in a brooder gets wet and messy, chicks might get *coccidiosis*, or *coccy* (COCK-see), a disease to which chickens are especially susceptible when young. Rations for baby chicks often contain a disease-inhibiting agent called a *coccidiostat* that greatly reduces the danger of this illness.

Chickens like to take *dust baths*, or thrash around in the dirt, raising a cloud of dust around their feathers to clean themselves and to discourage body parasites. Chickens have a *pecking order*, whereby they arrange themselves socially by rank.

With this brief synopsis of a chicken's world, let's go into the nitty-gritty details.

2

PROTECTING YOUR CHICKENS

Too many beginning chicken-keepers find out the hard way that chickens need to be fenced in. For one thing, you may want to protect your garden (not to mention your neighbor's) and other vegetation from the chickens. More important, you certainly want to protect your precious chickens from predators such as hawks, raccoons, skunks, weasels, cats, dogs, kids, and cars. We've heard many a sad tale of the disappearance of feathered pets. The following accounts offer examples of what happens when chickens are exposed to the cruel and hungry world.

GRIM TALES

We frequently see hawks flying around our area, and several times, we have managed to chase them away from our yard before they did any damage. But one year, before we put up a covered run, we witnessed a hawk carry off our little black bantam hen. One minute, she was happily scratching the soil nearby, the next minute, she was in the hawk's clutches, disappearing into the sky. Some of our friends with hawks living on their properties are certain that the raptors would never touch their chickens. Maybe, maybe not. Trust us—all it takes is one swift and sudden swoop to result in the loss of a beloved pet.

In earlier times, chickens commonly ran loose in people's yards, and, in some areas, you still see flocks foraging along the road. Initially, our own chickens ran loose in our yard, and occasionally a mother hen would take her

brood across the road to cultivate the neighbor's petunias. One day, an old farmer in overalls stopped his vintage pick-up, watched the chicks cross, and then drove on with a toothless grin on his face.

But, traffic can be hazardous to a chicken's health. Soon after we started raising chickens, we experienced rapid population growth in our area and the accompanying advent of fast-and-furious traffic passing our suburban home. Nowadays, drivers with patience and understanding are rare, and the traffic is so bad that we get nervous just crossing the road to the mailbox each day. To protect our chickens, and our own mental health, we constructed a proper coop with enclosed runs all around.

DOGS AND KIDS

People tend to believe that, if they raise their dogs and chickens together, the dogs will learn not to go after the chickens. One of our neighbors told us that his dog let little chicks play between his paws, and take naps under his chin. He said the dog even kept the chickens away from his unfenced garden. We were so impressed that we went out and got ourselves a puppy. We thought that we would train him to help keep our chickens in line. We thought that the puppy might also protect the flock by keeping away nighttime marauders, or at least alert us to them by barking.

All went well until he was about 4 months old. Then, one day, when we went out to feed the chickens, we found half a dozen recently killed cockerels lined up in neat order. We called the puppy over and told him how upset we were and explained that he mustn't do it again. The dog seemed to understand, and for some time didn't engage in any more chicken-killing. A few days later, we saw him chasing chickens again–this time with his tail between his legs. The puppy knew that what he was doing was wrong, but he simply couldn't resist.

In the long run, the neighbor, whose experience had initially encouraged us to get a dog, didn't fare well with his dog either. The dog got a bit too frisky with the chicks and killed some of them by accident. He was so ashamed that he buried the bodies. Our neighbor didn't know where his chicks had disappeared to until a few days later, when he came across the loose dirt.

And that dog went on to do more gruesome deeds. One night, he broke out of his yard, headed straight for our show bantams, and chewed the legs off several of our best hens. He was a canine Jekyll and Hyde.

As for kids–well, we never understood what they get out of it, but some children seem to find great fun in throwing stones at roosting chickens, or

chasing chickens around the yard until they're frantic with fright. Youngsters who help care for their family's flock usually develop a love and respect for the birds. But, the chickens might still need protection from not-so-well-behaved visitors.

We could write a whole book detailing the gruesome demise of various poultry pets of our friends and neighbors. Suffice it to say that a nice, strong pen will keep your flock safe from most such fates.

PROTECTING YOUR GARDEN

Aside from keeping your chickens safe, another good reason for confining them is to protect your yard landscaping and your garden. You can make chickens your helpers, if you work it right; but if given complete liberties in a garden, a flock of bantams or even just a couple of large chickens can devastate the vegetables and flowers in no time.

The first year we kept both a garden and chickens, we made the mistake of planting the tomatoes right outside the chicken yard fence, in full view of the flock. The sight of those luscious red tomatoes was just too much for the birds, and they persisted in finding a way, no matter how much wing clipping and fence patching we did, to get the ripe tomatoes before we did. They were watching those tomatoes ripen as closely as we were, but they got up earlier in the morning.

Chickens like to scratch around in the soil, and they don't care if the row of seedlings you just put out is in their way. They might uproot or bury the little plants, or they might gobble them up as they go scratching along.

Nevertheless, chickens and gardens can go well together, provided that the chickens are properly managed and controlled. Allowing the chickens to scratch in the garden between crops is an ideal way to reduce weed seeds and insect pests, and it also gives your birds exercise that helps keep them healthy. They may eat a lot of beneficial earthworms, but if you have good soil composition, the worm population will bounce back in no time. Our chickens like to be on the scene when we till the garden. As soon as they hear us start the til-

ler, they line up along the fence and cluck excitedly. If we let them into the garden, they follow along right behind the tiller, gleaning the goodies turned up by it.

Another trick for getting rid of garden pests is to lay boards in the garden plot, and then turn them over every few days and let the chickens in. You will get rid of a lot of slugs, earwigs, and sow bugs that munch on your garden at night and hide beneath the boards during the day.

You can allow a few chickens into the garden once the plants have reached a good size. They might nibble at your crops a bit, but they will reduce the pest population at the same time. Keep an eye on them, though, lest your whole

🐓 CHICKENS AND THE LAW

Before beginning construction on fencing and housing for your future chickens, check your local zoning regulations, municipal codes, and homeowner association rules. You may discover that there are legal restrictions on your chicken-keeping activities, such as whether or not you can keep chickens at all, and, if so, whether a license is required, how many chickens you are allowed to keep, how far from the property line and human dwellings they must remain, what kind of fence is allowed, construction methods that are and are not permitted, and so forth. Complying from the start is much easier and less expensive than a do-over later.

Garden party

garden disappear in a single afternoon. The number of chickens you allow into the garden with no ill effect on the crops depends a lot on what you plant and on the size of the garden plot. Some people keep bantams permanently in their gardens. Experiment–with caution.

BUILDING A CHICKEN FENCE

The ideal fence for containing chickens is a woven wire fence with small openings. You might think the best option would be chicken wire, also called poultry netting, which has 1-inch-wide openings woven in a honeycomb pattern, but, unfortunately, raccoons and other predators can rip right through chicken wire.

Better protection is offered by fencing variously known as yard fencing, lawn and garden fencing, small stock fencing, goat and sheep fencing, kennel fencing, and sometimes even poultry fencing. Suitable mesh size for chickens is either 2 inches square or 2 inches wide by 4 inches high. Suitable fence height for chickens is at least 4 feet. If you plan to keep a lightweight breed that likes to fly, or your area is rife with large predators like bobcats and coyotes that have no trouble leaping over a 4-foot fence, consider making it higher.

And, if you plan to cover the top of the run to keep your chickens from flying out or to protect

 **SIX BREEDS THAT FLY WELL**

American Game

Hamburg

Leghorn

Old English Game

Rosecomb

Sumatra*

*Gail's top pick

them from hawks, do yourself a favor and make the fence high enough that you won't have to crouch when you enter the run. A common and economical way to cover a run is with aviary netting. More expensive, but more secure, is hardware cloth or other wire.

Where such wild animals as rats, skunks, weasels, or raccoons are likely to burrow into the run, you might consider putting a wire bottom on as well. If the coop has a dirt floor, the bottom should extend under and around the coop, too. Use hardware cloth or other small-mesh welded wire placed deep enough not to interfere with dust bathing–about a foot should do. If you need more than one piece to cover the area, provide a good overlap and tightly fasten overlapping pieces together. Also fasten the wire around the outside edges to the bottom of the fence and to the inside walls of the coop. Then your chickens will be completely safe from preda-tors, and they won't be able to slip out under the fence by way of their own dusting holes.

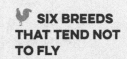 **SIX BREEDS THAT TEND NOT TO FLY**

Brahma

Cochin

Jersey Giant

Orpington

Plymouth Rock

Silkie*

*Gail's top pick

If you don't think that you need to wire the whole bottom of the coop and yard, you might sink some 1 by 6 pressure-treated boards all around the bottom edges of the fence, and attach the fencing to them. The boards provide a good solid bottom for the fence and somewhat discourage both burrowing in and digging out.

Chickens like fresh air and sunshine, but they know when they've had enough. When sunny space is limited, they will all try to get into a tiny patch of sunlight, and if the run is entirely exposed to sun, on hot days, they will crowd up in what little bit of shade they can find. So, be sure to provide for enough sunny and shady areas to keep them all happy. If possible, the sun should reach all parts of the run at some time during the day so the ground has a chance to dry rapidly following wet weather.

You may not want to construct a fence until after you have established housing for your chickens, but you certainly want to plan what kind of fence you will put up and where it will go. Otherwise, you may discover after your

Chickens love to dust themselves by lying on their sides and kicking up loose dirt. Dust-bathing serves to keep them clean and shake off some of the vermin that crawl on their bodies. Chickens favor certain dusting spots over others, and after a while the run will sprout several ankle-twisting holes, a situation you can prevent by providing bins of soft, loose soil or sand. Following a dust bath, a chicken often remains in the hole to bask in the sun, and can look decidedly dead lying there. If you spot a chicken in a hole, all spread out and lying still, check it out before you panic.

coop is built that its position in your yard doesn't allow for an adequate size run for your flock. A minimum yard size offers 10 square feet per chicken, although the more space you can provide for your birds to roam, the happier and healthier they will be.

A lot of chicken-keepers use a setup similar to ours. A secure chain-link fence surrounds our property and protects both our chickens and our apple orchard. Some days, we open the gate to the covered chicken run and let our flock free-range in the orchard. It's good for the chickens, and it's good for getting rid of apple tree pests. If you don't happen to have an orchard, you can let them roam your garden or lawn.

HOUSING YOUR CHICKENS

Before getting your first chickens, decide how you're going to house them. They will need a place to go inside at night, where they will be safe from predators, dry, and free from drafts. The shelter can be fancy or elementary. Where we had our first chickens, the yard was already equipped with a variety of odd structures that served as chicken housing. One looked like an old outhouse, modified with a chicken-size door toward the bottom for the chickens to go in, nest boxes at the back, and a perch for them to roost on. It was certainly simple and picturesque, and the chickens seemed to be entirely content with it.

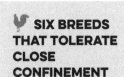

SIX BREEDS THAT TOLERATE CLOSE CONFINEMENT

Australorp

Belgian Bearded d'Uccle

Cochin

Silkie

Sussex

Wyandotte

Today, you can find a vast selection of ready-built chicken coops of various sizes and prices. Or you might be able to remodel an existing outbuilding to suit your needs. One way to gather ideas is to take a look at the different kinds of coops other chicken-keepers use in your area that work well in your climate. Most people will be delighted to show you their coops, and some areas organize annual coop tours. Regardless of the architectural design, certain features are essential to all coops.

COOP SIZE

The first consideration for coop size is to provide adequate floor space. If you plan to raise a large breed, at least 4 square feet will be needed for each bird. Bantams should not have less than 2 square feet each. The fewer chickens you keep, the more space they will need per bird.

Think about it: Let's say you plan to have three bantams. The coop size works out to be 6 square feet, or 2 feet by 3 feet. The birds will have barely enough room to turn around. And where will you find space for a feeder, a drinker, and a nest for the hens to lay in? On the other hand, suppose you plan to have 12 bantams. The floor space works out to be 24 square feet, or 4 feet by 6 feet. Plenty roomy enough for 12 bantams, and more than adequate for 3.

Chickens that are too closely confined get nervous and stressed out. The more flighty or excitable they tend to be as a breed, the more likely they are to pick on each other in overcrowded conditions. Some breeds simply respond better to confinement than others.

Here's another consideration: chicken math. Whatever number of chickens you start with, you're sure to become so enamored with your feathered pets that you'll want more. If your local regulations limit the number of chickens you can legally keep, consider building a coop to accommodate the maximum number allowed. That way, you won't find yourself soon building a second coop or an addition to your first coop.

If you purchase a ready-made structure, you won't have to do much calculating. Manufacturers specify the number of chickens each of their coop models will accommodate. They also make provisions for doors, windows, nest boxes, feeders, drinkers, and roosts. Some even include a fenced run.

A coop's height is mostly a matter of your own convenience. Chickens don't much care if their coop is 3 feet or 9 feet high. But, you might. You will need to frequently enter, or at least reach into, the coop to retrieve misplaced eggs, clean out litter and droppings, and catch the chicken that always seems to know when it is at arm's-length-plus-2-inches away.

If you decide on a walk-in coop, you'll be happier if it is tall enough to

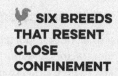

SIX BREEDS THAT RESENT CLOSE CONFINEMENT

Cubalaya

Fayoumi

Hamburg

Malay

Sicilian Buttercup

Sumatra

stand inside comfortably. Nothing is more miserable than cleaning out a coop on a hot, sweaty day with your head bent down because the coop is a few inches shorter than you are.

A smaller coop that isn't a walk-in should at least have an opening large enough that you can reach all the way into it comfortably. One of the original shelters that came with our house (and was quickly replaced) was shaped like a

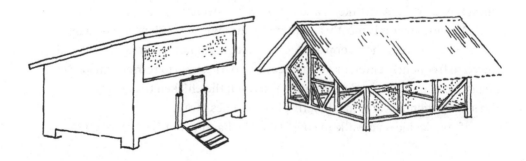

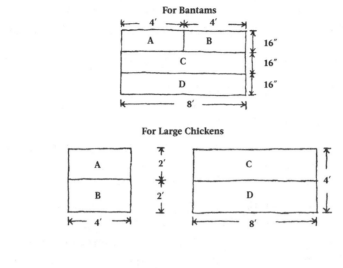

For Bantams

For Large Chickens

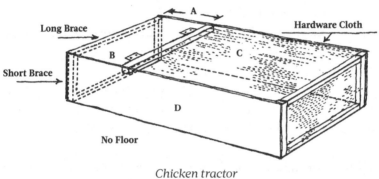

Chicken tractor

chest freezer, with the side walls just a little too tall to reach over with ease. We undoubtedly amused the neighbors to no end with our stand-on-your-head, wave-your-feet-in-the-air egg-retrieving and chicken-catching act. And, that coop was a real bear to clean out. Ease of cleaning is an important consideration, because a coop that's easy to clean is more likely to be kept clean.

ROOSTING BARS

Chickens instinctively seek an off-the-ground perch to roost on at night. Since they poop all night long, providing a perch for them to roost on is healthier than making them sleep on the floor.

Debate rages as to whether a perch should be round, like a bar for hanging clothing in a closet, or flat, like a 2 by 2, or a 2 by 4, with the wide side up. The chickens don't seem to care much either way. They will curl their toes around a round perch, or move toward the front of a flat perch and curl their toes over the edge. If you use lumber, round off the edges.

Observing that in nature chickens roost in trees, some keepers provide sturdy tree branches for roosting. Unsuitable for perch construction are PVC pipe, which is too smooth for chickens to comfortably balance on, and metal pipe, which is not only too smooth but also can lead to frozen toes in winter weather.

Install the perch far enough from the wall to allow the chickens to roost in comfort—at least 1 foot for bantams and 18 inches for large breeds. Allow 8 inches of roosting space for each chicken, 10 inches for the bigger breeds. Place roosts 2 feet off the floor. If you need more than one to accommodate all your chickens, space them at least 18 inches apart.

Some breeds like to roost higher off the ground than others. In fact, some of our bantams sleep in the coop's rafters. In a coop that's large enough to accommodate multiple perches, install them in stairsteps, 12 inches apart both vertically and horizontally. The chickens will start on the lowest rung and hop to higher rungs until they reach their comfort level. Fittingly enough, the highest-ranking chickens in the pecking order typically work their way to the top rung.

To confine nighttime droppings where chickens can't walk or peck in them during the day, install a droppings pit beneath the perch, and cover the pit with hardware cloth on a sturdy, removable frame constructed to hold the weight of the chickens without sagging—you may find that your chickens prefer to roost on the pit cover rather than on a perch. The frame should be easy to lift off so the droppings can be cleaned out frequently. Litter placed in the pit after each cleaning will help absorb moisture and keep down odor. Chicken manure is high in nitrogen and is great for the garden,

 SWINGING PERCHES

A swinging perch, suspended with chains, provides diversion during the day. Chickens, like children, like to play to keep from getting bored.

*Roost and droppings pit with removable
wire-mesh cover*

but use it only aged or composted, as fresh manure will "burn" growing plants.

ROOF AND FLOOR

The coop roof should be made of a material that will not absorb and hold heat. One of our coops came with a transparent green, corrugated plastic roof, which created an ovenlike effect in the coop on hot, windless summer days. Metal roofing or plywood covered with roofing shingles works fine. You may want to insulate the roof, if you are in an area that experiences extreme temperatures during the year.

A few small openings along the eaves will allow moisture to escape and provide fresh air, but be sure the chickens won't be roosting in a cross-draft. Chickens keep warm by ruffling up their feathers to create a thermal blanket that traps air warmed by their bodies. A draft blowing through the feathers will remove the layer of warm air, and protection on cold nights will be lost. Cover ventilation openings with hardware cloth to prevent predators from entering through them.

The floor can be quite simple if the coop is small—just make it one single droppings pit. In a larger coop, you'll want areas where you can walk. The floor should be one that will not collect and hold moisture, that is easy to clean, and that the chickens will not have trouble walking on.

A dirt floor fulfills most of the essential demands and, of course, is inexpensive to "install." On the other hand, it won't deter predators from digging into the coop from underneath, unless the soil covers a protective barrier of hardware cloth or other welded wire. A concrete floor is ideal, because it's easy to clean and impervious to predators.

A wood floor is a common option and, when covered with linoleum, is easy to clean. Make sure that the access to the space under the coop, between the floor and the earth, is sealed either with hardware cloth, wood, or a block footer, to prevent predators from taking up residence underneath. Spread litter on the floor wherever the chickens will be (as well as in the droppings pit) to absorb moisture and facilitate cleaning. Suitable types of litter include pine shavings, poplar shavings, shredded paper, well-dried chemical-free lawn clippings, and clean river sand.

DOORS AND WINDOWS

A coop needs plenty of ventilation to provide fresh air and to evaporate excess moisture from droppings, thus keeping the environment healthful. Besides ventilation openings beneath the roof, the coop should have doors or windows that may be opened during stifling hot summer days. Chickens cannot take high temperatures, and they will die if they get too hot.

When it comes to coop access, you and your chickens have different requirements. You could put in a people-size door and leave it open for the chickens during the day, but most chicken-keepers prefer to provide an additional small door, or pop hole, for the chickens' use. The coop we built to replace our original collection of chicken shelters has both people-size doors and chicken-size doors. For pop holes, we cut 12-by-18-inch openings in the sides of the coop, about 12 inches off the ground. The cut-out pieces became

Coop doors and ramps

the doors, hinged at the bottom and latched at the top. When open, they rest diagonally on the ground to provide a ramp into the coop. A few pieces of wood nailed crosswise provides traction.

Where predators are a threat, you'll want doors that can be closed and latched at night, after the chickens have gone to roost. The chickens will be protected from drafts, too. But don't forget to open them again the next morning. Just how early you have to open them will depend on how crowded the coop is and whether or not the chickens have access to food and water inside.

Sooner or later, most chicken-keepers discover automatic pop-hole door openers, of which several styles are available. Such doors have a light sensor that opens the pop hole at dawn and closes it at dusk, and some doors may be set on a timer to override the light sensor. An automatic chicken door opener will give you peace of mind, if you aren't Johnny-on-the-spot in letting your chickens out in the morning and locking them up at night, which can get to be a drag when life keeps you on the go.

One of our chicken-keeping friends had a coop situated at the edge of a forest. His chickens went into the coop each night, and he shut them in to protect them from forest creatures. One night, he forgot. Nothing happened, so he foolishly decided he didn't need to bother going out there after all. About a week later, all his chickens mysteriously disappeared in the night. An old saying states that experience is the best teacher. When the tuition is high, it's worth learning the lesson through someone else's experience.

NEST BOXES

Some kind of nesting boxes will be needed in the coop, at least one for every four hens. Nearly every publication on chickens lists specific measurements for nests, but we find that, as long as a hen isn't so crowded that she is uncomfortably cramped and likely to break eggs, and as long as she can get in and out with ease, almost any size will do. Use 12 by 12 by 12 inches as a minimum starting point, and look around for something you might repurpose, such as a pet carrier, a plastic bucket, an unused bureau—whatever. Be sure the nest is anchored, so it can't roll or tip over when a hen stands on it.

Nesting material should be fluffy and soft to keep eggs clean and prevent breakage. Pine shavings, sold at most feed and farm stores, are a popular option. The hens should be discouraged from roosting in the nests, which

causes the nesting material to soil rapidly and results in unsanitary eggs. A flap curtain hung in the nest opening helps prevent roosting on the edge.

Some hens like a ground-level nest, but most prefer an elevated one–up to about 3 feet high. Arranging the nests in a darkened, secluded area of the coop provides an enticing place for the hens to lay.

🐓 KEEP IT CLEAN

A fellow once visiting our coop asked, "How come your chickens don't smell?"

Surprised at the question, we responded "Why should they smell?"

To which he stated, "Chickens always smell." We suspect that's news to the chickens.

A chicken coop, to remain safe and sanitary, needs to be periodically cleaned out and disinfected. We clean ours twice a year, in spring and fall. Others, who use different management systems, clean theirs weekly or monthly. How often the job needs to be done depends on the number of chickens you have and what style of coop you have. Once you acquire your flock, you will quickly learn how often clean-out is needed to keep your coop pleasant for both you and your birds.

Begin clean-up by removing all fixtures, such as feeders, drinkers, and portable nest boxes. Then, remove the old litter and droppings. Scrape away any dried manure sticking to the various surfaces, and scrub the surfaces with disinfectant. A good chicken-friendly disinfectant can be purchased at most farm and feed stores. Dilute it according to the directions on the container, and use a hard-bristle brush or a broom to brush it onto all surfaces. Be sure to get it into all the cracks and crevices.

Choose a warm, dry day so the coop will dry out soon after you're finished. Removable fixtures can be placed in the sun, so they will dry quickly. When everything is clean and dry, apply the mite control of your choice (see the section on mites and lice on page 129), spread fresh litter on the floor and in the nests, and let the chickens back in to examine their clean digs.

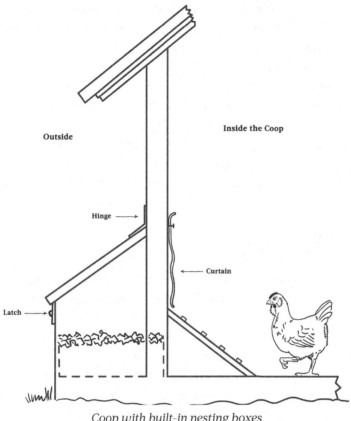

Outside

Inside the Coop

Hinge

Curtain

Latch

Coop with built-in nesting boxes

A handy way of arranging nesting boxes is to construct them so you can gather the eggs from outside the coop. The hens enter the nests from inside the coop, but you need only lift an outside lid to collect the eggs. Many ready-built coops use this system, especially those too small for a person to walk into. But, even with a walk-in coop, it's nice to be able to gather eggs without having to change (or clean) your shoes every time.

ADDITIONAL AMENITIES

Some coops are designed with extra space to store feed and chicken-keeping equipment. If you plan to include this feature, Chapter 5 will help you determine an appropriate amount of space for feed containers.

You might consider running electricity to your coop as well. A wired coop is especially desirable when winter weather may result in frozen drinking water, as well as frostbitten combs and wattles. When lighting is available, you will be able to stimulate egg-laying during the winter (as described on page 52). Lighting will also be convenient when you need to go into the coop at night. If wiring the coop isn't convenient, or if you opt for a portable coop, battery- and solar-powered appliances are readily available.

Do not be tempted to run an extension cord from your house to the coop, which can pose a serious hazard. We once visited a fellow chicken-keeper who had strung extension cords along the ground to power a variety of backyard coops and brooders. Shortly after our visit, we learned that one of the cords had frayed after being stepped on once too often and most of the coops burned to the ground, along with many beautiful chickens.

GOING HOME TO ROOST

You've gone through all the trouble of installing a nice, cozy coop. You bring your new chickens home, install them in the coop, and the first night, you discover that they prefer to roost in tree. Chickens that have been raised outside, especially bantams, usually prefer to perch in trees at night, and do seem to be the healthier for it–at least until they get nabbed by an owl or other night-time predator. Once they get into the habit of sleeping outside, they will continue to do so through rain, snow, wind, fire, flood, famine, and earthquake. However, it's much safer for them to spend nights indoors.

The best way to ensure this problem doesn't arise is to release the chickens inside the coop when you first bring them home, and leave them shut in for at least 3 days. After that, they will most likely return to the coop to roost every night. If, on the evening after letting them out, you find them attempting to roost outside, discourage them by shooing them inside as dusk approaches. Tossing a handful of scratch inside the coop usually serves as sufficient enticement for the chickens to scurry in.

After the flock has spent a few nights inside the coop, they will get the idea and go in of their own accord as the sun goes down. The old proverb about chickens always coming home to roost is quite literally true. All you have to do is to teach them where home is.

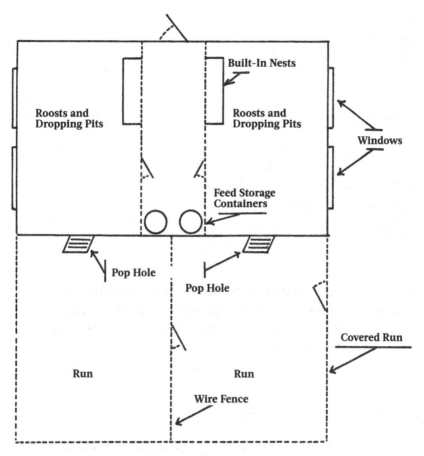

Built-In Nests

Roosts and
Dropping Pits

Roosts and
Dropping Pits

Windows

Feed Storage
Containers

Pop Hole

Pop Hole

Covered Run

Run

Run

Wire Fence

This coop design, which is similar to the walk-in coop we built to replace the conglomeration of structures we originally found in our backyard, allows a considerable amount of flexibility. It could house two different breeds from which eggs might be collected for hatching. Or one side could be used to house young growing chickens, while the other side houses the mature flock. Or the door between the two runs could be left open to provide maximum space for a single flock. Dimensions of the coop and runs depend on the number of chickens, with a minimum of 4 square feet per bird inside the coop and 10 square feet per bird for the run.

FEEDING YOUR CHICKENS

Chickens, like people, need a variety of nutrients in order to remain healthy. And, like people, they suffer serious nutritional disorders if certain constituents–including minute quantities of specific trace minerals–are missing from their diets. Also, their dietary needs change with age. Growing chicks have quite different needs than mature laying hens.

COMMERCIAL RATIONS

Commercially prepared chicken rations are designed to provide a perfectly balanced diet for each type of flock. A complete line of special-purpose chicken feeds, including formulations for baby chicks, growing fryers, growing pullets, layers, and breeders is available in many feed stores. Information on them may be found on the websites of major feed suppliers. The simplest feeding program, and the best option for the beginning backyard chicken-keeper, is to feed the flock the special-purpose feed that is designed to meet their needs.

Some feed suppliers offer a limited number of all-purpose feeds, for example a starter ration for chicks and a layer ration for mature chickens. In such a case, feed the starter ration to chicks for the first 5 months, or until they start to lay eggs, then gradually switch over to the layer ration. Do not feed layer ration to chicks before they are ready to begin laying eggs. Layer ration is lower in the protein chicks need for growth and higher in the calcium hens need to produce eggs. Chicks fed layer ration won't grow well and will suffer irreparable kidney damage.

Prepared feeds come in the form of mash, pellets, or crumbles. Mash consists of ground-up ingredients and looks something like cornmeal (but a different color). We find that both chicks and grown chickens tend to waste mash by spilling it on the ground and trampling it. Therefore, the pellet and crumble forms prove to be more economical.

Pellets are made by compressing mash into small tube-shaped pieces. Pellets are too large for baby chicks to eat but are ideal for mature chickens. Pellets come in a small size and a regular size, depending on the feed brand. We like the smaller size for bantams, and we also find that larger breeds spill less feed on the ground with the smaller pellets than when fed the larger size.

Crumbles are crushed-up pellets. Crumbles are best for baby chicks, with their small beaks. Some layer rations come as crumbles, but, again, we find that older chickens tend to waste more crumbles than they do pellets.

Rations are usually sold in bags weighing 25, 45, or 50 pounds, depending on the brand. Some feed stores will open a bag and sell feed by the pound.

Chicken feed is no longer cheap (even if it is still a metaphor for small-time financial doings), and when sold by the pound, the price can be outrageous. But feed does go stale and loses nutritional value. Purchase only as much as your chickens will eat within 2 to 3 weeks.

How much chickens eat depends on the season and the temperature (they eat more in cold weather than in hot weather), as well as their age, size, weight, health, and rate of egg-laying. We recommend keeping feed available to chickens at all times, a method called free-choice feeding, and let the chickens decide how much they need.

Incidentally, just because chickens get up at the crack of dawn doesn't mean you have to get up that early to feed them. Some of our friends assume we must be early risers because we have chickens, and they consider themselves at liberty to phone us at uncivilized hours of the early morning. But we just make sure some feed is out at sundown so the chickens can eat breakfast while we're still in bed.

HOW MUCH CHICKENS EAT*

TYPE OF CHICKEN	AMOUNT OF FEED (LB)	TIME PERIOD
Mature bantam	½	Week
Mature light (layer) breed	2	Week
Mature dual-purpose breed	3	Week
Mature heavy breed	4	Week
Broiler/fryer	10	Total in lifetime
*Approximate: varies with such things as breed, age, and ambient temperature.		

SCRATCH GRAIN

The old-favorite chicken feed called scratch consists of various whole grains mixed with cracked corn. It's called scratch because, when it's tossed on the ground, chickens come scrambling to scratch the ground, while gobbling down the grain. Scratch has been an old farm standby since time immemorial. But, it is not a complete dietary ration and makes an unsatisfactory permanent menu. That would be the equivalent of a human diet of doughnuts for breakfast, lunch, and dinner.

Scratch mixtures consisting largely of corn are not recommended. Some corn is fine, but as grains go, corn is lower in protein and higher in fat, and tends to make chickens obese. A plump bird is, of course, highly desirable. Plumpness results from full fleshing and is an excellent indicator of sparkling good health. But an obese hen doesn't lay well, and an obese fryer on the dinner table is unappetizing.

Scratch does have good uses. In cold weather, sending chickens to roost with a cropful of grain will help them stay warm, as the grain digests throughout the night. And, tossing a bit of scratch into the coop at sundown encourages reticent chickens to go inside, rather than spend the night in a tree or on the coop roof. Otherwise, think of scratch as a type of candy, and consider it to be no more than an occasional treat for your chickens.

NITTY-GRITTY ON GRIT

Chickens that are fed anything other than commercial poultry rations must have access to grit for their digestive systems to function properly. Since chickens do not have teeth, the masticating function is performed by their gizzards. The gizzard employs grit as a grinding agent. The grit may be simply pebbles and other small, hard indigestible objects the chickens happen to eat. Oh, and by the way, the reason chickens that eat only commercial feed don't need grit is that these prepared rations are sufficiently softened for digestion by the chickens' own saliva.

The grit itself gradually gets ground up, so it must be continually renewed. If chickens have a large outdoor area in which to roam, they usually get a sufficient supply of natural grit. For confined chickens, however, commercially prepared granite grit, which can be purchased at any feed store, will be necessary. Make a container of it available to your chickens at all times, so they can use as much as they need.

Another type of grit is calcium grit, usually in the form of crushed oyster shell. Laying hens need plenty of calcium to keep their eggshells nice and thick. A diet exclusively of layer ration supposedly supplies a sufficient amount, but the best laying hens usually need more than the ration provides. Therefore, make oyster shell available to them, especially if you are finding eggs with shells that are so thin they crack easily or that feel rubbery. These signs may indicate a calcium deficiency, and thin shells may encourage your hens to engage in egg-eating.

A lot of chicken-keepers like to recycle calcium by saving up eggshells and feeding them back to their hens. The shells should be well-washed, dried in the sun or oven, and crushed. Feeding chickens broken half-shells could well turn them into egg-eaters, and it is a hard habit to break. Their own shells alone do not provide hens with sufficient calcium for consistent egg production. Like granite grit, calcium grit eventually gets ground up and digested, so it should be available at all times for your hens to eat at will.

FREE-RANGE FORAGING

If a large, vegetative area is available for your chickens to roam, they will find excellent, nourishing, and delicious food. Seeds and insects will provide them with protein, as well as some of the essential vitamins and trace minerals that are so vital to a chicken's health. However, even on the best possible pasture, foraging chickens will obtain less than 5 percent of their daily nutrient requirements.

🐓 **SIX EXCELLENT FORAGERS**

Ancona

Andalusian

Hamburg

Old English Game*

Penedesenca

Welsumer*

*Gail's top picks

The amount of nutriment foraging can provide varies with the nature of the vegetation. The younger and more tender the shoots, the more protein they contain. Grass (from a lawn that has not been sprayed with toxins) are fine for chickens, since a lawn is generally mowed before the grass gets old and tough.

The older and tougher the vegetation, the more difficult it is to digest. Fibrous material can even become wadded up in a chicken's crop, blocking passage to the rest of the digestive system, a serious condition known as crop impaction that can end in the bird's death by starvation.

Granny had a catchy phrase to remind us of the proper type of vegetation to pasture chickens on: "The better for basket weaving, the worse for chicken feeding."

We plant kale around our coop to provide our chickens with greens throughout the winter. Kale is easy to grow and flourishes during mild winter months, providing a good supply of fresh greens that chickens love. Because the kale is planted near the coop, the chickens can help themselves. But we must protect the seedlings or the chickens will immediately eat the tender, young plants right to the ground. After the plants grow tall and develop thick stems, they are less likely to be destroyed.

Another good source of greens is sprouted grains. Chickens are particularly fond of sprouted oats. They also like salad scraps, weeds, and surplus or overripe fruit and vegetables from the garden, seeds and all. Cut larger fruits and vegetables in half or quarters, and be sure to sort out anything that has begun to rot, as it can make your chickens quite ill.

Like scratch, greens do not furnish a complete diet and should be fed in moderation. However, chickens love fresh greens, and pecking at growing forage, garden scraps, or sprouts gives them something to do to keep them out of mischief. Besides, as our neighbor keeps reminding us, our eggs taste "eggier" than the store-bought variety, and she really likes their rich, orangey yolks–a result of feeding the chickens fresh greens.

GROWING YOUR OWN FEED

Occasionally, we're asked about the practicality of producing homegrown chicken feed for backyard flocks. We have found that the amount of feed that can be raised in a small plot is hardly worth the time and trouble needed to grow it, and the monetary savings are virtually nil.

In an effort to economize and to provide our flock with especially fine feeds, we have attempted to grow grains in our garden. Our first crop was what we thought was a large patch of corn. After we watered and cultivated the patch all summer, and cut and dried the cobs in the fall, much to our dismay, the chickens got into the stored corn without our consent and gobbled it all down within one short afternoon.

Another year, we tried growing a plot of oats. The crop grew well, with little trouble to us beyond occasional watering. But, after the harvest, we found that the minute amount of grain we were able to recover was not sufficient compensation for the effort involved and for occupying a significant portion of our garden for an entire summer. Growing a substantial supply of chicken feed in a small area is simply not practical.

MIXING YOUR OWN RATIONS

Similarly, for the beginning chicken-keeper, mixing your own rations from purchased feedstuffs is equally impractical. For one thing, different types of chickens have different dietary needs. For another, all chickens have complex nutritional requirements. Too many novice flock-owners harm their chickens by attempting to mix their own feed, or by diluting a complete ration with all sorts of bizarre supplements that have been recommended by chicken-keeping friends or self-styled poultry gurus.

One of the biggest issues regarding home-mixed rations is providing adequate vitamins and trace minerals. Yes, vitamin and mineral premixes designed for chickens are readily available, but usually only in larger amounts than the average backyard flock-owner could possibly use within the premix's 6-month maximum shelf life. Using an outdated mix can result in serious deficiencies and sick or dead chickens.

As a beginning chicken-keeper, don't complicate things. And, don't play Russian roulette with your chickens' health by feeding recipes posted online

MAKE FEED CHANGES GRADUALLY

Avoid making any sudden or abrupt changes in your flock's diet. If you switch from one type of feed to another—for instance, when transitioning from starter ration to layer ration—make the change by mixing the two together and gradually increasing the percentage of layer ration until the changeover is complete. A rapid change in feed can result in serious digestive upset for your flock.

by people who most likely don't have the first clue about poultry nutrition. Find a brand of commercial ration that works well for your chickens, and make that the primary source of nutrients for your flock.

FEEDING FACILITIES

Feed should be stored in tightly covered containers. Depending on how much feed you purchase at a time, you might store it in a 5-gallon bucket with a lid or in a clean container designed for collecting garbage. The container will protect the feed from both rodents and moisture. Moldy feed should never be given to chickens, as it can make them seriously ill.

Using feeders is more sanitary than tossing the feed on the ground where the chickens walk and poop. Many different types of feeders are available from feed stores and online. Each style has proponents and detractors. Options include troughs that attach to a wall, freestanding troughs, hanging

A treadle feeder is a popular option

feeders, treadle feeders, rain-protected range feeders, and more. As chicken-keeping becomes ever more popular, new feeder styles are invented every day. The style that works best for you will depend on the size and number of your chickens, the space available for a feeder, and whether you plan to install the feeder inside or outside the coop.

Features to watch for are, first of all, ease of cleaning. A feeder should be emptied and cleaned at least once a week. The easier this task is accomplished, the more likely you will be inclined to do it.

Another important feature is a method to keep chickens from roosting over, and pooping in, the feed, as well as stepping or scratching in the feed, or taking dust baths in it. Some feeders have either a wire guard or a cover designed to discourage roosting. Another option is to use a narrow feeder attached directly to the wall, which won't give the chickens enough room for roosting.

Yet another important feature is one that prevents chickens from flicking feed onto the ground with their beaks, a habit called *beaking out.* Feed that's been beaked out is rarely eaten, but instead gets trampled and pooped on and can attract rodents. A rolled-in lip on a trough feeder will discourage beaking out, as will filling the trough only half full. A style of feeder that requires chickens to poke their heads inside the feeder also prevents beaking out.

If you plan to install your feeder outside the coop, it should have a cover to keep out rain. It should also have a method for making the feed unavailable to rodents and poultry predators during the night. If nothing else, bring the feeder indoors at night and return it to the yard in the morning. Wild birds, and especially pigeons, may be attracted to an outdoor feeder, and their pilfering can significantly up your feed bill. The solution to this problem is to keep the feeder in a covered run.

FRESH WATER IS ESSENTIAL

Plenty of fresh, clean water must be available to chickens at all times. This essential aspect of poultry nutrition cannot be overemphasized. A large chicken will drink between 1 and 2 cups of water a day, depending on the weather. A chicken cannot drink much at once, so it must drink often, and it will do so where water is readily available.

Chickens must have water to be able to digest their feed. A chicken is more than 50 percent water, and eggs are 65 percent water. A hen that doesn't get enough water cannot lay well. Even if she is deprived of water for only a short time, her laying may be seriously impaired.

Puddles of stagnant water from rain or leaky drinkers should be eliminated so the chickens won't drink from them. Puddles become fouled by the chickens' excrement, making them an ideal breeding medium for harmful bacteria and other disease-causing organisms. Chickens are not at all choosey about where they get their drinks. In fact, even when fresh clean water is available, they'll still gravitate toward puddles. The quality of their drinking water is therefore only as good as the poorest water available.

As with feeders, a wide array of drinkers is available, ranging from bell-shaped waterers and automatically filling water bowls to nipples attached to water pipes or buckets. In selecting a style, consider the climate and whether or not the same type of drinker may be used year-round. You might opt to use one style in summer and a different style in winter, when the weather freezes. Or you might get an extra waterer, so you can bring the frozen one inside to thaw, while the chickens are using the other one. Or you might consider getting a drinker with a built-in heater for winter use.

Plastic versus metal is a consideration when purchasing a bell waterer.

One type of automatic waterer

Homemade nipple drinker

Both materials have poultry-keeping proponents. Galvanized metal drinkers are more durable than most plastic ones, and they resist deterioration by sunlight, but they can rust fairly rapidly. Plastic won't rust, and it's noncorrosive, but it is more likely to crack if the water freezes. Plastic is also more susceptible to getting moldy and accumulating algae; therefore it requires more frequent cleaning.

In choosing a bell waterer, select a style that won't tip over easily; otherwise, the water must be replaced frequently, and a wet floor provides a good culture for disease-causing organisms.

Living in a mild climate, where freezing weather is rare, we equipped our coop with automatic watering devices. They are easy to install on accessible faucets or with a length of inexpensive plastic pipe. You could also use a length of hose, if you get the type intended for potable drinking water. Once the waterers are installed, they are easy to maintain, if you clean them regularly to prevent algae from growing and remove any bugs or bits of dirt that have slowed the flow.

Many chicken-keepers today use nipple drinkers, which may be installed directly on a water pipe as an automatic device, or may be attached to a bucket or other container that is periodically refilled. Properly installed nipples don't leak or need constant scrubbing to keep them clean. You just have to check them daily, by tapping each with a finger, to make sure it isn't clogged.

Having chickens is no fun if their maintenance becomes an unpleasant chore. The amount of daily care chickens require, however, is minimal if you get properly set up and work out a daily routine of feeding and watering. Using feed and water equipment that best suits your climate and your flock's needs will go a long way toward simplifying your daily chores and giving you more time to enjoy the company of your healthy, contented flock.

ROOSTERS TO CROW ABOUT

We are asked so many questions about roosters that we decided they rate a chapter of their own. The question we hear most often is "Do I need a rooster?" Well, unless you want fertile eggs to hatch, you really don't. The rooster has nothing whatever to do with whether a hen lays eggs or not. Furthermore, not even a chicken psychologist can say for sure if a rooster keeps the hens happy. It seems to us, actually, that hens are more relaxed without a rooster around to harass them. Let's face it, roosters are the original male chauvinists. The common use of the word "cocky" reflects how outrageously arrogant their behavior can be. However, roosters are half the fun of having

🐓 COCK OR ROOSTER?

In poultry exhibition circles and on chicken-breeding farms, a mature male chicken is called a cock. Most everyone else calls him a rooster. The word "cock" comes from the Old French word *coc* (in modern times, *coq*), meaning male bird. Eventually, the word evolved into roost cock, meaning a male bird that roosts.

The word "cock" also evolved as a reference to young men who strut around like a cock, and eventually became a synonym for a lecherous person. When the word took on a more direct sexual connotation, the puritans changed the term for male chicken from *roost cock* to *rooster*. So even though male and female chickens both roost, the word "rooster" applies only to male chickens, not to hens.

chickens, and watching the full spectrum of social interaction in an integrated flock is nothing short of fascinating.

COCK AND HENS

Listening to a cock talking to his hens is an enchanting experience. If he finds a tasty morsel crawling along the ground, he may pick it up and throw it down several times—an activity known as *tidbitting*—to make sure the hens see it, and cluck excitedly for them to come and share it with him. The sound he makes is the same as mother hens make to call their chicks, and it is clearly an important part of chicken talk. Sometimes, however, a cock will turn tidbitting to his own advantage, fraudulently enticing a hen to him for less-than-honorable purposes.

Dancing rooster

A rooster does a little dance number for hens that turn him on, in which he skitters sideways, spreads his wing feathers downward like Japanese fans, and flicks the tips of his wings against the ground while moving in a semi-circle around the hen. If he's particularly fond of you, he might do this little dance for you when you pay him a visit. Don't confuse this courtship dance with the aggressive stance, in which a rooster sidles up to you sideways just before he launches an attack against your legs.

Unlike some other bird species, chickens don't pair off. However, certain cocks have preferences for certain hens, always sharing their goodies and clucking endearments throughout the day. When a cock believes that the hens in his harem are ranging dangerously far, he'll call them back to his side.

ROOSTER AS PROTECTOR

The rooster will protect his flock, occasionally attacking when he believes that a member of his harem is being harmed. We've been threatened now and then by a normally friendly rooster when a hen we were carrying set up a squawk. This behavior can be an advantage in discouraging predators, especially when you have a setting hen, whose primary concern is protecting her eggs. The cock will in turn protect the hen. An article in our local newspaper once described an unsuspecting eagle that brazenly marched into a coop looking for a chicken dinner and was beaten to a bloody pulp by the rooster in charge.

That the word "chicken" has become synonymous in our language with coward is entirely unfair. Admittedly, chickens have a well-developed sense of discretion about when to run. But, more than once, we've seen roosters heroically put their lives on the line to protect their communities.

Roosters are always on the lookout for hawks and will sound an alarm whenever they see one—or anything vaguely similar, like a biplane or a butterfly. They can be quite suspicious. Or paranoid. Or alarmist. But the rest of the flock will take the alarm seriously: The other cocks immediately join the Chicken Little falling-sky chorus, and the hens and chicks all dive for cover. You can easily identify the hawk alarm, because, remarkably enough, the cry sounds almost exactly like a drawn-out "Hawk!" in English.

Roosters will rarely attack a person, even with provocation, especially the person they belong to and see every day. If you insist on being afraid of them, anyway, do not assume that the larger ones are invariably the fiercest. Quite to the contrary, a feisty little banty cock can be formidable, while a rooster of a larger breed may be quite mellow. In any case, roosters ordinarily reserve their rancor for each other.

Once in a while, a rooster might get cranky and become aggressive toward you. You can usually head off future attacks by picking him up (when he's not being aggressive) and showing affection, such as stroking his wattles or the feathers on his back. The wrong thing to do is to be physically aggressive with the rooster, such as giving him a swift kick or squirting water in his face. That only serves to incite him to future violence in his attempt to show you who's boss.

Every now and then, an ornery rooster comes along that just has a mean streak, plain and simple. We advise against keeping a rooster that continues to attack you or anyone else. Despite any advice you might find online about how to tame a persistently mean rooster, do yourself a favor and get rid of him before you, a family member, a neighbor, or a young child gets seriously injured.

COCK-TO-HEN MATING RATIOS

PER COCK OF THIS SIZE	OPTIMUM NUMBER OF HENS	MAXIMUM NUMBER OF HENS
Bantam breed	18	25
Light breed	12	20
Heavy breed	8	12

TOO MANY ROOSTERS

Should you decide to include roosters in your backyard flock, the next question is likely to be "How many should I have?" If fertile eggs are your main purpose in having cocks, then you need to start by knowing the mating ratio for your breed, which tells you how many hens one rooster can reasonably handle. A rooster of a bantam or other light breed can fertilize the eggs of more hens than a rooster of a heavy breed, and an older rooster can handle only half as many as a young cock.

Since some cocks may tend to have certain favorites among the hens, eggs from all hens still may not get fertilized, even if you have an ideal rooster-to-hen ratio. And you never know which eggs are fertile and which aren't until you've set them to hatch for about a week, by which time the infertile ones are no longer good for eating. So, since roosters are pretty anyway, and since one may lay his life on the line for his hens, it doesn't hurt to have spares.

On the other hand, quite often, two roosters in the same flock will fight more than if the flock includes three or more roosters. And, if your small flock has too few hens to justify keeping more than one rooster, have a backup plan in case something happens to him and you need a replacement. For most breeds, roosters are far more plentiful than hens and therefore are easier to come by.

Whatever your purpose, you don't want more cocks than hens running in the same pen. For one thing, the roosters will do more laying than the hens, and the poor hens will be run ragged. For another, cocks with competitors among them will fight more, and they could be so busy fighting each other

🐓 TREADING

When a rooster mates a hen, he grabs her head feathers in his beak to help balance himself while he stands on her back. Typically, his feet will slide against the smooth feathers on her back, and he'll try to get a better grip with his claws. This action is called *treading*, and it can result in the significant loss of feathers from the hen's back. A hen with missing feathers has little protection from the cock's sharp beak and claws, and future matings can result in serious injury.

The hen lowest in pecking order is usually mated more often than other hens and therefore will be the first to lose her feathers. As soon as you notice your hens start missing feathers because of treading, or even before feathers go missing, take any or all of the following measures:

- Trim the rooster's toenails using a pair of pet toenail clippers or human nail trimmers, and finish by filing away sharp corners.
- Separate the rooster(s) from the hens, joining them together only one day a week—the average duration of fertility after a single mating is 10 days.
- Temporarily outfit your hens with breeding saddles, widely available online.
- If a hen becomes injured, separate her from the rest of the flock and treat her wound until it heals.

that no eggs will get fertilized. A curious thing happens, though, if all the hens are removed from the pen; fighting among the cocks ceases almost entirely.

COCK FIGHTS

SIX AGGRESSIVE BREEDS

Cubalaya
Modern Game
Old English Game
Rhode Island Red*
Sumatra
Wyandotte*

*Some strains

Even a reasonable number of cocks will fight occasionally. If you bring a new rooster into the yard, a fight will ensue between him and any cocks-in-residence to determine the new pecking order. Unless the new rooster is particularly strong, the established cock fiercely defending his established territory will generally win. The fighting should subside once the new cock has found his place. When roosters are reunited after a separation, they may fight, even though they formerly coexisted peacefully.

A rooster's place in the pecking order is dependent far more on his age than on his size and vigor. Fights are mostly bravado and strategy, and the outcomes are largely determined by psychology and experience. Fights between cocks already living together usually occur only when a young upstart challenges one of his elders. The older cock will usually win unless he is feeble or quite old and his authority is waning. But if the younger cock is persistent, he will win in time.

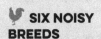

SIX NOISY BREEDS

Andalusian
Cornish
Cubalaya
Leghorn
Modern Game
Old English Game

So, fighting is normal and not much to worry about. Usually, the roosters will settle things for themselves and stop fighting before mortal wounds are inflicted. But if two cocks fight perpetually and inflict serious injuries on each other, one should be permanently removed from the flock.

Incidentally, hens sometimes fight with the younger and weaker cocks or with each other. We've never seen this challenge become serious, and their big show of bluff can be quite amusing.

COCKS WILL CROW

The most characteristic thing about roosters is their crow. Nearly everyone has an opinion about it, too. Some people refuse to have a cock around, because they feel it disturbs the peace. Others insist on having one, just to hear it crow. A fellow we know named his rooster Reality, because of his early-morning wake-up call.

For some people, hearing a cock crow in the morning is a pleasant experience. An old fellow stopped by our place one day to see if we had any spare roosters. We took him out to the coop, and he listened intently until one of our roosters crowed. With a gleam in his eye and a grin on his face, he pointed to the crowing bird. "That's the one I want," he said, and scuttled off clutching his prize. That rooster was his only chicken—his bit of country life.

A chicken-keeping friend of ours once had a hassle with his city council over his crowing roosters. When asked if there wasn't some way to keep the cocks from crowing, he cracked up all those present with his drawled reply: "Well, there is one operation that will prevent them from crowing, but, unfortunately, it also prevents them from breathing."

Actually, it is possible to have a rooster's crower surgically removed, but most veterinarians don't know much about it and won't attempt it. You would have to go to a specialist, and, even then, decrowing would be extremely expensive, not to mention risky and not always successful.

Since crowing has become an issue in suburban areas, some enterprising person invented a so-called anti-crowing collar. We don't recommend this device, because the line between crow prevention and strangulation is far too thin.

Another friend of ours kept roosters in town, much to the annoyance of his neighbors. To prevent legal hassles, each evening, he put the roosters in crates and stacked the crates in the shower stall in his spare bathroom. In the darkened room the roosters were less inclined to crow, and with the shower door and bathroom door closed, if they did crow, the sound was muffled enough to avoid complaints.

It's a myth that roosters crow only at sunup. The truth is they crow anytime they feel like it. The only thing that can be said with certainty is that they crow up a storm in the morning. But they continue to crow intermittently throughout the day, and sometimes even at night.

Crowing in the dark of night is usually triggered by some outside stimulation, maybe from a light shining on or near the coop—say, the headlights of a passing car, a porch light snapped on, or a burglar's flashlight. A rooster might also crow if it's disturbed by something or somebody moving in or close to the coop, if it hears a loud noise, or if it hears another rooster crowing in the distance.

One cock awakened by a passing car can get every rooster in the neighborhood crowing. Usually it doesn't last long, and they all soon go back to sleep. When we first had chickens, we would wake up whenever a rooster crowed at night, but now, it's just become part of the normal night sounds and doesn't disturb us a bit—unless one of our roosters has gotten loose and decides to perch on the bedroom windowsill when the sun rises.

(7)

EGGS FROM YOUR HENS

The age at which a healthy pullet (young hen) will lay her first egg depends, in large part, on her breed. Breeds that have been developed primarily for high egg production may start laying soon after they reach 4 months of age. Many backyard breeds start laying at about 5 months. Slow-maturing breeds may not lay until the age of 8 months, or even later.

EGGS ON THE WAY

A pullet that is ready to start laying eggs will display distinct signs. She will be nearly full size for her breed and will have grown a complete set of shiny adult plumage. Just before she starts to lay, her small, pinkish comb will get larger and redder. She may begin to sing or otherwise become more vocal. She will begin checking out possible nesting sites, peering into dark corners of the coop or wandering in and out of nest boxes, maybe even sitting in one for a short time as a sort of trial run.

You may be looking forward to your first omelet, but the bird's purpose in laying eggs is to produce chicks. A pullet that is about to start laying will therefore instinctively want her eggs to be fertile. If a rooster approaches, she will crouch down to be mated. If your flock has no rooster, the pullet may crouch for another hen, or for you.

 **SIX TOP LAYING BREEDS**

Ancona

Campine

Fayoumia

Leghorn

Rhode Island Red*

Sex Link hybrids*

*Gail's top picks

The pullet's pubic bones–the pair of pointy bones located between the breast and the vent–will increase in flexibility and spread apart to make room for eggs to pass between them. By the time a pullet is ready to start laying, you should be able to place at least three fingers between her pubic bones, or two fingers if she is a small breed. When laying starts, she will develop a soft, deep abdomen and a large, moist vent.

LAYER LONGEVITY

Hens are at their peak from 1 to 2 years of age, and are considered to be old by 4 or 5 years of age. But those of us who get attached to our hens want to keep them around, and you might find that you still get plenty of eggs to about 4 years–and we know of hens as old as 9 years that are still laying.

Nevertheless, you must expect fewer eggs as your hens age, and, if your purpose in keeping chickens is to provide eggs for your kitchen, consider growing out a few pullets each year to avoid a sudden decline in egg production. Otherwise, you might end up like a friend of ours, who jokingly complains about running a home for geriatric hens.

The life expectancy of a well-cared-for hen is 10 to 15 years. However, chickens rarely die of old age. Most backyard birds are dispatched by unnatural causes, such as predators, disease, culling, or being served at the dinner table.

Depending on which breeds you have, you can expect approximately an egg every day or two from each hen during her laying season. Industrially developed hybrid hens are bred especially for egg production, so they lay better than most purebreds. Hens of exhibition breeds, on the other hand, are bred for beauty more than functionality and may lay precious few eggs.

Hens stop laying now and then for various reasons, many of which are not cause for concern. Moving the hens to an unfamiliar location, changing the feed or feeding routine, and extreme or sudden changes in temperature can all cause a temporary interruption in the laying pattern. For example, sometimes laying will stop for a short time during the warmest part of the summer.

The most common reason for reduced laying is the autumn molt, when hens need all the energy they can muster for renewed feather growth. Then they often take a nice, long rest through the colder weather. Like autumn leaves, their combs lose their luster and remain dull and shrunken during the nonlaying period. When the hens are ready to lay again in the spring, the vivid color will return to their combs. A few hens may start laying right after the molt and continue to lay throughout the winter months.

It is, however, irregular for laying to stop during mild weather. Since eggs are about 65 percent water, an inadequate water supply—in winter, when water freezes, or in summer, when hens drink more and it may run out more often—can cause a decrease in laying. Also, make sure your hens are getting an adequate diet. Hens on a poor diet cannot put nutrients into both laying eggs and maintaining good health. Make sure that the chickens' diet includes sufficient protein, as well as supplemental calcium. Internal or external parasites are another possible cause. If the problem persists, the hen may have a disease (see Chapter 13 for more on health issues). Or maybe she's simply getting on in years.

If fluctuations in egg-laying can be expected from backyard chickens, you may wonder why eggs are available in markets year-round. Well, industrial producers use only hens bred specifically for egg-laying, and they regulate the feed, temperature, and lighting in their henhouses to ensure maximum production. Such high-producing hens tend to wear out early in their lives, so they have to be replaced often; most industrial producers don't keep a flock of mature hens for much more than a year.

COLLECTING THE EGGS

It's a good idea to collect eggs two or three times a day. Frequent collection keeps eggs from getting broken by subsequent hens coming into the nest to lay and helps prevent egg-eating. It also keeps the eggs from being chilled or overheated during weather extremes. Further, predators may be attracted to nests if eggs remain in them overnight.

Most hens lay their eggs in the morning. The process of producing an egg takes about 25 hours, causing a hen to lay her egg about an hour later each day. Since a healthy hen doesn't lay during the night, eventually she'll skip a day and start laying again the following morning.

Hens will generally lay their eggs in the nesting boxes provided for them, but, occasionally, they need the encouragement of fake eggs in the boxes. Fake eggs may be purchased at some farm supply stores, department stores, import shops, and hobby shops and are available just about anywhere at Eastertime. Golf balls work fine as fake eggs, too.

Our first dummy egg was a white stone egg we received as a joke one

Christmas. It looks so real that when guests help us collect eggs, they invariably make some puzzled comment about "that awfully heavy egg."

Later, we found a store that had stone eggs of all colors and had fun picking out some wild ones to plant in the nests. The chickens seem totally oblivious to the colors, so long as the egg is round and feels good. The theory behind using fake eggs is that, when a hen sees eggs already in the nest, she will decide it must be a safe place for eggs and deposit hers alongside.

Hens lay eggs in the oddest places. A hen's first egg, which may be quite tiny, will often be laid on the ground wherever she happens to be standing when the urge strikes. It seems to catch her by surprise, and she doesn't quite know what's happening. But, after the first one, she usually gets the idea and heads for a nest next time.

Banties are especially fond of hiding their eggs. If you think you aren't getting all the eggs you should, look around for a hiding place–under a bush, behind the nesting boxes, or in a hollow tree. If you have hens that like to play this kind of game, consider leaving a fake egg in place of the eggs you take. Otherwise, the hen may look for another place to lay that may be even harder for you to find.

Sometimes, a banty hen will fly over the fence to lay her eggs in the bushes or weeds and then fly back into the run. We've found piles of eggs in places we hadn't even known chickens had been. A hen will occasionally disappear altogether and, just about the time we think we've lost her, she'll come strutting back with a brood of peeping chicks following behind.

 **EGG COLOR**

Eggs come in an assortment of colors, varying from white to pink to blue to green to nearly black. Eggs laid by any single hen may usually be identified by their hue. A friend of ours once had a hen that laid pink eggs with purple spots. Egg color is influenced by breed, but even within a single breed, some variation occurs. Rumors to the contrary, the color of the shell has no bearing on the nutritional value of the contents.

SIX LAYERS OF COLORED EGGS

BREED	SHELL COLOR
Araucana	Blue
Ameraucana*	Blue
Barnevelder	Dark brown
Easter Egger hybrid	Pastels
Olive Egger hybrid	Olive
Marans*	Darkest brown

*Gail's top picks

EGG BINDING

Occasionally, a hen may get egg-bound, which means there's a "traffic jam" in her oviduct, and she could die as a result. Just because a hen stops laying and appears uncomfortable, don't automatically assume she's egg-bound. She may be ill from some other cause. An egg-bound hen will be sluggish and ruffle her feathers, her abdomen will distend, she will strain as if trying to lay an egg, and you will be able to feel eggs inside or maybe even see an egg protruding from the vent.

Coat your finger with a water-based lubricant such as K-Y Jelly and gently insert it into the vent as far in as you can reach. Another option is to gently squirt in warm soapy water using a syringe without a needle. Sometimes, greasing or soaping up the works helps ease the way for a stuck egg.

If that doesn't work, warm up the egg-laying muscles and maybe the hen will relax enough to release the egg. Moisten a towel in hot water, or place a damp towel in a microwave just long enough to make it warm, but not hot, and hold it against the hen's vent area for about 15 minutes, rewarming the towel as needed. If the egg doesn't come down on its own, rest a few minutes and try again. Standing the hen in a tub of warm water is another way to try to relax her.

Occasional egg binding may occur in winter, when a hen's egg-laying muscles may be cold and a little on the stiff side. Or it may happen when a hen lays a big double-yolker or a pullet lays a large egg before her system is ready to handle it.

A hen that is persistently egg-bound has a serious problem. She may have some disease that causes swelling or loss of muscle tone. Her diet may be calcium deficient. She simply may be too fat, a common issue with pampered backyard chickens. Although occasional egg binding may be easily resolved, there's not much hope for a persistently egg-bound hen.

 EGG SIZE

Egg size depends on the hen's breed. Large breeds lay bigger eggs than bantams, and some large breeds lay bigger eggs than others. A pullet's eggs will be smaller than a hen's, and small eggs are sometimes laid during summer hot spells.

SIX LAYERS OF EXTRA-LARGE EGGS

BREED	SHELL COLOR
Delaware	Brown
Jersey Giant	Brown
Minorca	White
New Hampshire*	Brown
Orpington	Brown
Rhode Island White	Brown

*Gail's top pick

FERTILE EGGS

A common fallacy is that fertile eggs have higher nutritive value than infertile eggs. In truth, there's no significant difference. Furthermore, whether or not a fresh egg is fertile cannot be determined without cracking the egg open.

All eggs have a small white spot on the yolk called the *germinal disc* or *blastodisc*, which usually may be seen when the egg is cracked into a pan. This spot is where fertilization takes place, but the spot is there whether the egg is fertilized or not. With a close examination, you can distinguish between a fertile and an infertile egg. If the spot is irregular and disorganized, and appears entirely opaque, then the egg was not fertilized. If it is neat and rounded with a small translucent eye in the center, like a tiny bull's-eye, you are looking at the beginning of a baby chicken. A blastodisc that's been fertilized is called a *blastoderm*.

On opposite sides of the yolk are two white lumps, which are actually twisted cords of thick egg white that protect the yolk by centering it within the shell. When you break an egg, these cords snap away from the shell membrane and recoil against the yolk like two little white knots, giving the cords their name from the Greek word *khalaza*, meaning small knot. One cord is a chalaza, two are chalazae. Chalazae are sometimes mistaken for the blastoderm. We have a friend whose aunt won't eat an egg when the chalazae are clearly visible, because she knows "what that hen has been up to."

Blood spots are also sometimes mistaken for a developing chick. A blood spot is the result of a minor hemorrhage that may occur when a yolk is released from the hen's ovary. Although such spots are quite common and harmless, you won't find them in commercially sold eggs, because the eggs have been candled (see page 79), and any with blood spots have been removed. The only reason for discarding eggs with spots is aesthetic: That is, some folks are finicky.

EGG CLEANLINESS

If nesting litter is kept clean and nests are not used for roosting, eggs should remain clean. Unless absolutely necessary, avoid washing the eggs. A freshly laid egg is coated with a moist outer membrane–you may see it if you happen by moments after an egg is laid. This coating, or bloom, dries right away, forming a barrier that retards moisture loss and prevents bacteria from entering the egg.

The bloom is removed when an egg is washed, and the egg's keeping ability is thereby greatly reduced. Removing the bloom is of concern if you plan to hatch the egg or if you store it for any length of time before eating it.

An egg that's coated with mud or manure is unsafe to eat and should be discarded. When an eggshell is slightly soiled, try to brush or scrape the dirt off. If you feel an egg absolutely requires washing, observe these four important requirements:

- Clean the egg soon after gathering it.
- Wash the egg in water that is warmer than the egg.
- Include detergent or bleach as a sanitizer.
- Use the egg right away.

EGG STORAGE

A common practice outside the United States, and a growing practice among American chicken-keepers, is to store eggs on the kitchen counter instead of in the fridge. Eggs that are clean when collected and remain unwashed to preserve their protective bloom may be safely stored on the kitchen counter for up to 2 weeks. However, consider this: According to the American Egg Board, an egg ages more in 1 day at room temperature than in 1 week in the fridge. So quality-wise, those 2-week-old countertop eggs compare to eggs that have been in the fridge for 14 weeks. And, isn't the reason for keeping hens in the first place to enjoy their fresh eggs?

We prefer to put eggs we're going to eat into the refrigerator as soon as possible after collecting them. In the fridge, they will keep for 5 weeks or more, but, as they age, the white loses its firmness and the yolk may break when the egg is cracked. You can usually tell how fresh an egg is by how much it spreads when cracked into a skillet. The fresher the egg, the thicker the white will be and the more the yolk will stand up. Because these qualities also depend on the chicken's heredity, diet, and state of health, if an egg you know is fresh exhibits characteristics of a stale egg, consider other management issues.

A freshly laid egg has no pocket of air, or air cell, at the blunt end. When the egg cools, and the contents shrink within the shell, a small air cell develops. As the egg ages, moisture evaporates through the shell, causing the contents to continue to shrink and the air cell to expand. So an older egg has a larger air cell than a fresh egg. The cell may be examined by candling or may be measured indirectly by immersing the egg in water. A fresh egg sinks. An aging egg stands on end with the blunt end upward. An old egg floats. Discard the floaters.

We have found that really fresh eggs are difficult to peel when hardboiled, but, if they are boiled after the air cell has expanded over a few days, the shells come off more easily. This is one case where freshness is not necessarily a virtue.

Freezing eggs is a good way to handle the summer egg surplus and provide for the winter shortage at the same time. Properly frozen eggs are much like fresh ones in appearance, flavor, and nutritional value. Freeze only perfectly fresh eggs, which will keep for 9 months to a year at 0°F or lower.

Eggs to be frozen should be removed from their shells, because the contents will expand and the shells will burst. One way to prepare eggs for freezing is to scramble them and add 1 teaspoon of honey or ½ teaspoon of salt for each cup of eggs, to keep the yolks from getting pasty; then pour the eggs into

Four ways of serving eggs: with corned beef, poached, Benedict, and soft-boiled

ice-cube trays. Remove the frozen cubes from the trays, store in plastic freezer bags, and thaw as needed. Use thawed eggs within 24 hours. Though eggs vary in size, for recipe purposes, one egg is roughly equal to one cube from the ice tray or about 3 tablespoons.

If you so desire, you can separate the yolks from the whites before freezing them; while salt or honey must be added to the yolks so they won't get gummy, the whites will be fine without any treatment. Each egg equals 1 tablespoon of yolk plus 2 tablespoons of white.

Fresh or frozen, the eggs from your backyard flock will provide you with ample resources for such exotic culinary treats as eggs Benedict, eggnog, custards, hollandaise sauce, and homemade mayonnaise. Let your creativity run wild with those amazing golden nuggets of protein.

THE SETTING HEN

In no portion of the life cycle of chickens is the role of instinct so important as in the hatching of fertile eggs by a setting hen. Humans understand the mechanics of procreation so thoroughly that we have a hard time putting ourselves in the position of a chicken, which plays out its role in the drama of life and death only in response to certain urges, and without the vaguest idea of what it's doing or why.

THE URGE TO BROOD

Hens, we must suppose, have no suspicion that an egg is a potential chick. Still, laying seems to be a relatively emotional experience for a hen—the ultimate high of bird-dom. When a hen has the urge to lay an egg, she apparently begins to feel how nice it would be to find a secluded place to sit in for a while. If she can find a place that already has some eggs, so much the better. She doesn't realize she is both assembling a clutch and hiding it from predators.

Yet, if either of these functions had been omitted, the chicken would never have been known to humans, for it would never have endured all those eons of survival of the fittest. Of course, the system is not perfect, and not all hens have equally strong instinctive urges. Some breeds never get broody, but mechanical incubators make up for that. Hundreds of times more eggs are laid than ever turn into adult chickens under natural circumstances; and it's a good thing, too, or the world would long ago have drowned in chicken feathers.

Likewise, when a hen decides one warm spring day to remain in the nest, she has no idea that the warmth and humidity of her body provide just the

FEATHERLESS BROOD PATCH

To keep her eggs warm during the incubation period, a setting hen loses the insulating feathers from an area on her breast. The featherless skin thickens and develops additional blood vessels that bring the hen's warm blood closer to the skin's surface. Known as the *brood patch*, the purpose of this featherless area is to bring the hen's body warmth in closer contact with the eggs and to keep the eggs from drying out too fast, by lending moisture from her body. Once the chicks hatch, the hen's breast feathers grow back.

right conditions for the eggs beneath her to begin developing into chicks, that by leaving the nest briefly each day to eat she gives the eggs a much-needed cooling period, and that when she returns and wiggles around in the nest to get comfortable, she inadvertently performs the essential task of turning the eggs.

She sits night and day in a trance, snuggling the eggs to her. But, by hatching time, she's just about tired of it all; and, so, although the sudden transformation under her from eggs to chicks surely comes as somewhat of a surprise, it does seem to be a refreshing experience, and she's simply tickled to death. She immediately develops an amiable relationship with the new-comers, and enjoys cuddling them in her feathers or hustling them around in search of choice tidbits.

If, by chance, the eggs are infertile or for some other reason fail to hatch, she will, in time (perhaps another week or two), tire of the whole game, come out of her trance, abandon the nest, and resume her normal activities. It's not that she realizes it would be futile to remain on the eggs, but simply that, from her point of view, setting loses its charm after a time. Just as the decision to set in the first place is instinctive, so also is the decision to stop. In this way, nature prevents hens from wasting energy on a lost cause.

PREPARING FOR SPRING

Living in a mild climate, we prefer to hatch chicks early in the season–from the time egg-laying gets into full swing until the beginning of summer. In northern areas, it would be better to delay hatching until the weather warms up. Eggs may be available year-round, but the fertility of the parent stock is greatest in spring, and, in general, the overall quality of the chicks will be greater.

We find that chicks hatched late in the season tend to be smaller, not as vigorous, and slower growing compared to early chicks. Besides, the later in the season they hatch, the greater are the chances that growing birds will not have matured enough to withstand cold or rainy weather. Hens that get broody and attempt to set late in the season should be firmly discouraged from setting.

If you have several breeds running together most of the year, and you want to raise chicks whose lineages you control, the first step to take as the hatching season approaches is to separate the breeds before eggs are to be collected for hatching. Although the average duration of fertility is about 10 days, to be on the safe side, allow 4 weeks for sperm to clear from random breedings. If you are raising show stock with the hope of breeding top prizewinners, be especially careful to keep track of the breeding. Of course, if you don't mind raising mixed breeds, you won't have to worry about this step, but be aware that when bantams and large breeds run together, after a few years of hatching their eggs, you will end up with a lot of mid-size chickens.

Although a flock should be free of mites and lice at all times (page 129), checking for these vermin in the spring and eliminating them before any chicks start to hatch is especially important. An extreme case of body parasites may kill a setting hen and certainly will kill baby chicks.

COLLECTING EGGS FOR HATCHING

Fertile eggs remain dormant until they are incubated, whether naturally or artificially. It is nature's way of allowing a hen to accumulate a clutch of eggs until she's serious about setting, ensuring that the resulting chicks will all hatch at the same time. That's the reason humans can store and eat fertilized eggs without fear of consuming a partially developed chick. It's also the reason that we can accumulate eggs intended for artificial incubation.

Some chicken-keepers who want their hens to set stop collecting eggs and leave them all in the nests, hoping the hens will take the hint and become broody. But we think this practice is a waste of eggs. Left in the nests, the eggs may get broken or soiled, or the weather may be cold enough to freeze the eggs or warm enough for the embryos to begin partial but harmful development. On the other hand, when eggs are collected and properly stored for hatching, they may still be eaten. So if no hens go broody, your eggs won't have gone to waste.

Store eggs saved for hatching pointed-end down in a cool, draft-free place. Nature permits a period of dormancy in eggs to allow a hen to collect a clutch together before she starts to set, so all the chicks will hatch at the same time. A temperature as close as possible to 55°F will keep the embryos dormant. Neither store them in the refrigerator nor try to keep them warm; an embryo will die at temperatures below 40°F and may begin to decompose at temperatures above 60°F.

We get best hatching results if we don't hold eggs for more than 7 days before setting them, although they may be kept for up to 14 days with some hatching success. To keep yolks from sticking to the insides of the shells, turn the eggs by tilting the cartons from one side to the other daily. Tilting is easily done by elevating one end of the carton one day, and the opposite end the next day.

Eggs retained for hatching should be from healthy, vigorous stock. Select eggs that are all the normal size and shape for their particular breed and that have thick shells with no cracks. Oversize or oddly shaped eggs seldom hatch. Smallish eggs will produce small chicks, but, eventually, they are likely to catch up with chicks of the same breed from larger eggs.

🐓 THE EGG SEXING MYTH

Predetermining the sex of a chick that will hatch from any given egg is not possible, despite what some chicken "guru" might try to tell you to the contrary. A friend once gave us some eggs to hatch and told us, "I knew you'd want hens, so I brought you only the eggs that are going to hatch into hens." When we asked her, with veiled skepticism, how she knew, she gave us a demonstration: A set of keys held over an egg will soon start to swing—longitudinally if a rooster will hatch from the egg and transversally if a hen will hatch from it. This feat is, of course, due to magnetic forces coming out of the egg, she said. She got it straight from Mother Goose. If it were possible to sex eggs by this or any other means, commercial hatcheries could save a fortune by setting only eggs of the sex they need—pullets of laying breeds and cockerels for broiler production.

Mark each egg with the date (and breed, if you have more than one) when it is picked up. A wax pencil works well for marking eggs: It's easy to read, won't rub off during the normal course of the hatch, and isn't as likely as a pencil or pen to puncture the shell. We don't care for fluid markers, as the ink might soak through the shell and possibly contaminate the egg or embryo. The reason for dating the eggs is to keep track of exactly how long they have been stored; in the event a hen doesn't get broody in time, you'll know which eggs are still good for hatching, which are only fair for hatching, and which are still safe to eat.

We don't know of any way to force a hen to become broody, although the following tricks have been suggested as ways to encourage broodiness to some extent.

- Provide darkened, undisturbed nests near floor level.
- Furnish clean, soft nesting material.
- Place dummy eggs in the nests to give the appearance that eggs are accumulating.
- Play sound recordings of peeping chicks (and let us know if this one works).

You can tell you have a broody hen when she stays on the nest, ruffles her feathers, growls at you, and pecks your hand if you try to move her or take her eggs. She will set on fake eggs, or she may even stay on an empty nest. We had one hen that tried to hatch three little green apples she carefully rolled into her nest when they fell from an apple tree!

A setting hen seems almost hypnotized throughout the brooding period, maintaining a dreamy, vacant-eyed look. She will get rather possessive about her eggs, carefully tucking under herself any that roll out of position, and can become decidedly nasty about defending her eggs against any moving thing that comes anywhere near.

Each hen follows a pattern in her setting habits. When you get to know your hens, you will be able to predict fairly accurately when each is likely to set, and how dependable each is as a setter and as a mother. Some hens never set. Chickens bred exclusively for high egg production necessarily have had the brooding instinct bred out, although individual hens may occasionally miss that memo.

To be reasonably certain to have hens that will set, obtain a breed known to be especially dependable setters and good mothers. Many breeders of exotic birds use Silkies for hatching, because they have a strong instinct for setting and caring for their brood. Cochins also have strong brooding instincts, as do common barnyard bantams.

We've had people inquire about buying a broody hen. A hen can be broody in one place and change her mind by the time she's moved. So if you're lucky enough to find someone willing to sell you a broody hen, consider yourself doubly lucky if she continues to set once you get her home. To help ensure that she will continue to set, move her at night and set her on dummy or unwanted eggs until you're sure she's still so inclined.

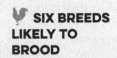

SIX BREEDS LIKELY TO BROOD

Brahma
Cochin*
Dorking
Old English Game
Orpington
Silkie*

*Gail's top picks

SIX BREEDS UNLIKELY TO BROOD

Andalusian

Lakenvelder

Polish*

Spanish*

Sultan

Sicilian Buttercup

*Gail's top picks

BROODING FACILITIES

One year, we had three hens all setting on the same nest, literally one on top of the other. One of the hens was somewhat larger, and it was comical to see the other two peering out from under her wings like overgrown chicks. The eggs hatched into 22 baby chicks, which the three hens took collective care of. At night, the little ones went under whichever hen had the most room. We called them the commune.

This experience happened to turn out well, but we haven't always been so lucky. Sometimes, two or more broody hens fight over the eggs, to

---

 BREAKING UP A BROODY

Some hens should not be allowed to set, even if they do get broody, either because they are not reliable during the incubation period or because they do not take proper care of their chicks once they hatch. Or maybe you want to continue collecting eggs and, therefore, don't want your hens to set.

To prevent a broody hen from setting, you could try to break her up. Since egg-laying terminates when a hen gets broody, the sooner you break her up, the sooner she will start laying again. Depending on how determined the hen is, one or more of the following measures may work.

- Take all the eggs away.
- Repeatedly move the hen off the nest.
- Move or block the nest.
- Move the hen to a different environment.

Since a brooding hen loses a considerable amount of weight, persistent brooding can be decidedly detrimental to the hen's health. A stubbornly broody hen can actually starve to death. If you have a hen that persists in brooding despite your best efforts to break her up, put her in a broody coop, which is little more than a wire cage without a nest or bedding. Provide feed and water, and keep her in the coop as long as necessary to break up her broodiness—typically 1 to 3 days.

the detriment of the eggs. Or often, when a setting hen leaves the nest momentarily to eat, another hen decides to contribute her egg to the clutch, confusing the setter when she comes back and finds someone has taken her place on the nest. If the broody hen decides to settle on another nest, her original eggs will chill and be ruined after the interloper finishes depositing her egg and leaves.

To avoid mix-ups between broody hens and nonbroody layers, prepare separate places where each setting hen will be alone and away from the general flock. A nest for a hen to hatch her chicks in should be roomy enough to allow her to move around a little and turn her eggs; it should contain enough nesting material for the hen to settle in and keep the eggs warm; and it should be placed where the chicks will be safe when they hatch and are ready to explore—for example, you don't want them to fall into a droppings pit and not be able to get back up to their mother.

The portable chicken tractor described on page 20, with a nest box added, provides an excellent place for isolating a setting hen. When moving a broody hen, follow the same precautions as for purchasing one: Move her at night, and give her a few eggs you don't care about until you are certain she will continue to set in her new location. A hen that is not serious about her job of hatching chicks is wasting her time and your eggs.

THE COUNTDOWN

Once you have determined that a hen is serious about setting, put the eggs you want hatched under her, but don't give her so many that any stick out around the edges. If one sticks out and gets chilled, she'll rotate it back in and leave another out to chill until the whole batch might be lost.

We find that 8 to 10 eggs under a banty, or 12 to 15 under a larger hen, is plenty, but it also depends on the size of the eggs relative to the size of the hen. A bantam can handle fewer large eggs than she could eggs of the size she lays. Note the date when you place the eggs, and expect your new chicks in 21 days. Depending on factors too numerous to mention, not all the eggs may hatch.

A setting hen leaves the nest infrequently to eat, drink, and eliminate, so don't be alarmed if you see your setting hen off the nest. When she returns, in settling back into the nest, she will rearrange and thus turn the eggs. She will generally return within 30 minutes, though a bit longer won't endanger the

🐓 EARLY COMMUNICATORS

Because chicks are able to scurry around and feed themselves soon after they hatch, they run the risk of being separated from their protective mother hen. To avoid this danger, they must immediately learn to recognize the sound of her voice. Communication between the setting-hen mama and the embryos still enclosed within their shells ensures that baby chicks will recognize the sound of their mother's voice from the moment they hatch.

eggs. After the first few days, however, a long period of cooling will kill the developing embryos. In such a case, either the hen was delayed–perhaps somehow being barred from returning to her nest–or she is seriously thinking of giving up the job.

On the other hand, if your setting hen is not getting off the nest at all, be sure she has plenty of food and water within reach. The first thing a broody hen does on leaving the nest is to relieve herself of an enormous poop she's been saving up for the occasion. A hen that doesn't leave the nest eventually can't hold it any longer, fouling the eggs. Feeding her only scratch grains (no layer ration) will keep her droppings more solid and help prevent her eggs from getting soiled.

When her eggs get close to hatching, the mother hen starts clucking to them as if they've already hatched. For this reason, a setting hen or mother hen is often called a *clucker*. The embryos within the eggs will peep in return. Mother and offspring are getting acquainted, even before the hatch.

FOSTER MOTHERS

If you don't have a rooster, but you want to raise chicks, you could purchase some fertile eggs and set them under your broody hen. She won't know the difference and will hatch them as if they were her own. But be sure to give

them to her fairly soon after she has begun to set; a hen kept on the nest much more than 21 days may lose interest and decide to quit. Tips and cautions on purchasing eggs for hatching may be found on page 139.

You could even set eggs of other poultry species under your hen. She won't care, and she will mother anything that hatches under her. But she may be alarmed if her babies jump into a pond and start swimming around. On the other hand, she just may jump in and swim right along with them.

Some eggs, such as duck, goose, and guinea eggs, take longer to hatch than chicken eggs. Although we've seen many cases where hens have hatched them successfully, sometimes a hen won't sit it out that long. If you don't have another broody hen waiting in the wings, you might try to line up an incubator to move the eggs into, just in case. And, don't try to set a huge goose egg under a little bitty banty hen, or a clutch of tiny fragile quail eggs under a klutzy New Hampshire hen.

When a hen sets on infertile eggs, or no eggs at all, the natural culmination of the brooding period will not occur. In such a case, if you have access to freshly hatched chicks, you may wish to give them to the hen to mother, even though she didn't hatch them herself. Wait until the hen has been setting for at least a week before giving her chicks. If you think the eggs she's on could be fertile but haven't started hatching, wait until day 22, in case they're late hatchers.

Although it's possible for a hen to accept a batch of chicks without the preparatory brooding period, it's also possible she will ignore them, or even kill them. A hen is more likely to accept the role of foster mom if she's put in the mood for motherhood by being allowed to set a spell.

Not only must the hen accept the chicks but also, just as essential, the chicks must be snookered into accepting the hen as Mom. Timing can be critical in getting this to happen. The younger the chicks, the better the chance they will recognize and identify with the hen you have selected as their foster mother.

To increase the chances of mutual acceptance, slip the chicks under her at night. While you're at it, remove whatever she was setting on. Oh, and you needn't leave eggshells strewn about the nest to complete the charade.

Watch carefully the first day and, in the event that the hen will not accept the chicks, be prepared to mount a rescue. Whether a hen hatches the eggs herself or is conned into raising chicks hatched elsewhere, we're always prepared to gather up the young and raise them ourselves. For whatever reason, young birds of certain species–guineas, peafowl, and some duck breeds, for example–don't always respond to the hen's motherly clucking and will wander off motherless and helpless.

THE NEW BROOD

By whatever means she acquires them, the mother hen will take care of the chicks once she accepts them, and you needn't do much, other than to make sure they are in a safe place with plenty of fresh water within their reach, and something suitable to eat. The easiest plan is to feed them all a starter ration. The hen will eat it, too, so be sure to provide enough to go around. High-protein, low-calcium starter won't hurt the hen, as she won't resume laying for another couple of weeks, but layer ration, with its high level of calcium, will certainly harm the chicks.

For at least the first month, keep the hen and her chicks isolated from the rest of the flock. Confining the young chicks will prevent marauders from getting at them, as well as protect them from being pecked by some of the other chickens. For some reason, the big guys can be pretty mean to the little ones. Mother hens will even peck a chick from another hen's brood, if it gets too close.

We once made the mistake of attempting to save space by putting two

mother hens with their broods together in one small coop. Soon, one of the hen's chicks were getting weak and listless, while the other brood was thriving. After watching a while, we discovered that one mother had claimed the territory that included the food and water containers, and she wouldn't let the other hen's chicks near them. Luckily, we rectified that situation in time for the hungry chicks to regain their strength.

For a newbie chicken-keeper who is completely unacquainted with the nature of birds, the first hatch can be a traumatic experience. A college student who acquired a mother hen with chicks from us called a few days later to complain that the chicks were not doing well. It turned out that she hadn't been feeding them, but she blamed the hen. She said she learned what the problem was when she checked the hen's breast, and discovered the hen's milk had dried up. We discreetly pointed out that chickens are not mammals, and therefore do not have mammary glands.

MECHANICAL INCUBATING

Leaving incubation to a hen is always easier, and those that stick it out have uncanny success. But some hens are just not reliable, and when you've lost a few clutches to an incompetent hen, you may prefer to turn to artificial incubation. Or maybe you become involved in a conservation project to help safeguard the continuation of a rare breed. You might want to incubate eggs just so you can enjoy watching the fascinating process by which a chick extricates itself from the shell after growing within for 21 days.

 SIX RARE BREEDS

Ayam Cemani*
Crèvecoeur
La Fleche
Redcap
Spanish
Yokohama

*Gail's top pick

HATCHING EGGS

Collecting and storing eggs for incubation is the same whether you intend to use a hen or a mechanical device: Hatch in the spring, separate different breeds, select the best eggs for high hatchability, mark eggs with date and breed, store the eggs in a cool place but not for too long, and so forth, as described on page 62. Don't be tempted to simply stick every egg into the incubator as it is laid. You will soon see that collecting eggs over a period of time and putting them in all at once makes keeping track of your hatch much easier, and also increases the likelihood that your hatch will be successful.

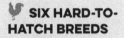

SIX HARD-TO-HATCH BREEDS

Araucana

Dark Cornish

Japanese

Minorca

White Wyandotte

Serama

Extremely soiled eggs carry harmful bacteria and should not be put into the incubator. Slightly soiled eggs may be cleaned with fine sandpaper or a dry sanding sponge. Like many backyard hatchaholics, we don't put "dirties" in our incubator, and we find that washing reduces hatchability, so we simply dispose of soiled eggs.

How successful you are at hatching in a mechanical incubator will depend on a large number of factors, including egg fertility and cleanliness, proper egg storage prior to incubation, the health of your breeder flock, the inherent degree of difficulty in hatching your chosen breed, and how carefully you follow the instructions for your particular incubator.

INCUBATOR OPTIONS

Mechanical incubators for home use range from tabletop models designed to hatch three eggs to cabinet models that will hatch hundreds at a time. Some incubators have clear tops or sides to provide a view of the entire hatch. These models are especially nice for classroom use.

Because incubators come in such a wide variety of styles, operating instructions vary. The key to success is to follow the manufacturer's suggestions for the incubator you have. This chapter will explain how an incubator operates in general terms. However, this explanation is not intended as a substitute for the manufacturer's manual.

Incubators for home use are either of the forced-air (fan-ventilated) type or the still-air (gravity-ventilated) type. Forced-air incubators provide better control over hatching conditions, because a fan keeps the warm air circulating, so the temperature remains constant. These incubators come in all sizes. Less-expensive still-air incubators have a heating element that's close enough to all of the eggs to keep them a uniform temperature, and, therefore, this type of incubator comes only in tabletop models.

The incubator should be operated in a room with a constant temperature of about 70°F. It should not be located near a window, near a heater, or in

Two styles of tabletop incubators

direct sunlight. A forced-air incubator will usually operate properly even when the conditions in the room are less than perfect, whereas more caution must be used with the touchier still-air incubator.

You'll want to frequently check the incubator to make sure everything is working right, so locate it where monitoring will be convenient. On the other hand, keep the incubator out of the main stream of traffic, where nobody can trip on the cord and accidentally unplug it, as happened to a friend of ours who didn't discover the dangling cord until several days too late. Our own first cabinet incubator looked much like an old-time refrigerator, and we were always afraid a visitor might open it looking for a cold beer.

Most of today's incubators have highly accurate digital controls. Still, you can't expect to consistently hatch 100 percent of fertile eggs. A reasonable expectation is 85 percent. Consider any more than that to be a bonus.

INCUBATION TEMPERATURE

Most of today's poultry egg incubators are factory preset for chicken eggs and are generally operated at 99.5°F. Until you gain experience using a particular model, avoid adjusting the temperature setting. With experience, however, you may possibly improve your hatching rate by tweaking the temperature setting slightly up or down.

A digital incubator has an LED display that tells you the temperature and other conditions within the incubator. Less-expensive models require the addition of a thermometer, designed specifically for use in an incubator. The thermometer most likely will be included with the incubator, and replacement thermometers are available from poultry suppliers that offer incubators and parts. With a good incubator thermometer, you should be able to detect a temperature change of 0.5°F.

Turn on the incubator for at least 24 hours to give it time to warm up before setting the eggs. Expect the temperature to drop when you put the eggs in, but it will gradually return to operating level as the eggs warm to proper temperature.

POWER SPIKES AND OUTAGES

When using an electronic incubator, protect it with a surge protector. Otherwise, frequent power spikes and surges will wear down the incubator's electronic system. A single high-voltage spike or surge could destroy it and easily put an end to your hatching season.

An outright power failure may or may not affect the hatch. An outage of 12 hours or less will likely do little harm. Early in incubation, cooled embryos naturally go dormant, and, during late incubation, the activity of hatching may generate enough heat to withstand a short-term outage.

An outage of 18 hours, on the other hand, may delay the hatch and could significantly reduce your success rate. If your eggs are especially valuable, consider having a standby generator at the ready, or know where you can get one in a hurry.

Incubator thermometer

INCUBATION HUMIDITY

Proper humidity during incubation prevents excess loss of natural moisture from within the eggs. Most incubators have a water pan from which moisture evaporates to regulate humidity. Some pans are divided into sections; the more sections you fill, the more the surface area is increased from which evaporation occurs, and vice versa. Other incubators use humidity pads to help regulate humidity. A few select models have built-in humidity regulators that work automatically, as long as water is available in a provided container.

The drier the air inside the incubator, the faster moisture will evaporate from the eggs through their shells. Conversely, the moister the air, the slower moisture will evaporate from the eggs. Too high or too low humidity can prevent chicks from emerging from the shell during the hatch or cause abnormalities in those that do manage to hatch.

Low humidity may result from a too-small water container or opening the incubator too often. During the hatch, it may occur when the water's surface gets coated with chick fluff, impeding evaporation. High humidity most often results from either poor incubator ventilation or high ambient humidity. If droplets of water accumulate on the incubator's observation window, the humidity is too high.

A digital incubator generally indicates the humidity level in an LED display. Less-expensive models do not have a built-in hygrometer, in which case, the changing size of air cells in the eggs may be used as a moisture indicator, as explained on page 81. The proper humidity level at various stages of incubation for your particular incubator should be explained in the model's instruction sheet.

TURNING THE EGGS

A handy feature for any incubator is an automatic turning device. Eggs need frequent turning during incubation, and without an automatic turner, you'll have to do the job by hand—at least three times a day—to keep the developing embryos from sticking to the shell membrane. A setting hen turns her eggs instinctively while nestling on the eggs, to ensure adequate contact with her brood patch.

If you have to turn the eggs by hand, do it at evenly spaced intervals. To help us remember, we turn ours right after breakfast, on getting home from work, and just before going to bed. If you can work it into your schedule, more than three daily turnings would be better, but make it an odd number, so on consecutive days, the position of the eggs during the long overnight periods will alternate. Avoid turning at irregular intervals or missing a lot of turnings in a row.

A handy way to turn eggs is by rolling them with the palm of your hand. To be sure you've turned all the eggs all the way over, mark an X on one side of each egg and an O on the opposite side. After turning, all the eggs should be either Xs or Os. Wash your hands well before turning, so your body oils and dirt won't get on the eggs and seal up the pores, and wash your hands afterward to avoid the possibility of spreading bacteria.

An incubator with a turning rack keeps eggs properly spaced. Place eggs in the rack, pointy end down. When an incubator lacks a turning rack, you might be tempted to overfill the incubator, but crowding makes hand-turning difficult and can reduce the hatch by providing insufficient space for the emerging chicks to maneuver out of their shells. So don't be tempted to set more eggs than the manufacturer specifies. Position the eggs with the pointed ends slightly downward or level, but not higher than the blunt end.

When a chick hatches, it should break through the blunt end of the egg, where the air cell provides oxygen until the chick cracks all the way through the shell. Chicks pipping the small ends of the shells means that the smaller end did not remain lower than the larger end during incubation. As a result, chicks become restricted by the shell and may fail to hatch.

Eggs should be turned from the 2nd to the 19th day of incubation, or 3 days before the eggs are expected to hatch. Then, stop turning the eggs, to give the chicks time to orient themselves and figure out where they are going to pip and unzip the egg.

EGG CANDLING

After 1 week of incubation, and again just before turning stops, candle the incubating eggs to see that they are developing properly, and discard those that aren't. Years ago, candling was done with a candle, which is how it got its name, but these days, we use an LED pocket flashlight. In a darkened room, hold an egg against the business end of the flashlight, and you will see what's going on inside the shell. Eggs with colored shells are more difficult to candle than white-shelled eggs, and speckled eggs are most difficult.

During the first candling, if you see a tiny dark spot with spiderweb-like veins running out in all directions, you're in business. If the egg is clear, it is either infertile or the embryo died early. If the yolk appears as a dark shadow

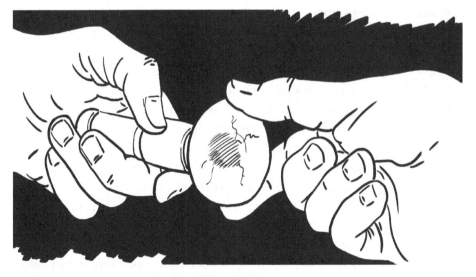

Candling an egg

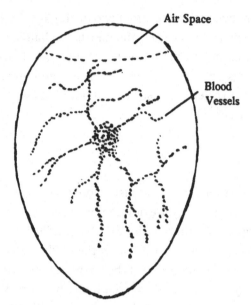

Air Space

Blood Vessels

Fertile egg, one week after incubation

or you see what looks like grayish clouds, the egg is rotting. A blood ring, which looks like a thin dark circle around the inside of the shell, indicates that the developing embryo has died. Embryos may die for any number of reasons, including the egg was too old for incubation, the storing temperature was wrong, or the incubator temperature was irregular.

Spoiling eggs give off harmful gases and use up oxygen that is better saved for the properly developing eggs. Once in a great while, a rotting egg will explode, sending out a spray of gooey, stinky stuff that's not only a huge mess to clean up, but will contaminate the other eggs as well. So remove any eggs that aren't developing properly.

Rarely will every egg hatch that is incubated, and so many factors are involved that it is sometimes impossible to determine exactly why. Among other things, the vitality of the parent stock could be low due to poor diet, old age, disease, or heredity; the hen-to-rooster ratio could be too high or too low; the eggs could have been stored incorrectly or for too long; or the incubator could have been operated improperly. Exact details for operating an incubator vary with the type of incubator used and the breed of eggs incubated, so a bit of technique-tweaking can often improve future results.

CANDLING TO MONITOR HUMIDITY

Candling eggs during incubation can tell you if the humidity is right. Compare the air cell in the blunt end of the egg to the diagram below. If the air cell is larger, humidity is too low; if smaller, humidity is too high.

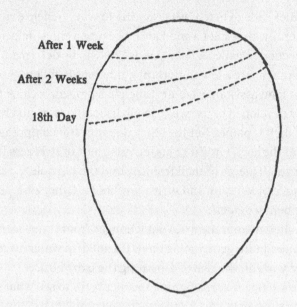

After 1 Week

After 2 Weeks

18th Day

WOO-HOO! HATCHING TIME

Even though we've hatched a good number of eggs, we still get excited each time we hear peeping sounds coming from the incubator. Chicks usually hatch on the 21st day after the eggs are placed in an incubator, although that can vary somewhat. Eggs that were held a little longer than usual before being set, or that were incubated under a slightly low temperature, will take longer to hatch, while those incubated under a slightly high temperature will hatch a little sooner than usual, as will eggs that had a head start because a broody hen had been setting on them before they were collected. Large eggs–such as those laid by a Jersey Giant hen–can take as much as 2 days longer than normal, while smaller bantam eggs tend to hatch a day or two early. Eggs laid by the smallest bantam, the Serama, may take only 17 days to hatch.

Eggs of the same kind that are all set at the same time should all hatch around the same time–within about 24 hours after pipping begins. If a lot of chicks pip without actually hatching, most likely, the humidity is not high enough. Sadly, when the humidity is too low during the hatch, the shell membrane dries and hardens soon after the chick pips, trapping the chick inside the shell.

When a chick fails to hatch, it's tempting to want to help extricate it from the shell. Generally, that's not a good idea, because a chick helped out of the shell–fittingly enough called a *help-out*–is likely to be deformed. But if you just can't resist, here are a few important guidelines to follow.

1. Do not lend assistance before a shell has pipped. A chick that is too poorly developed or too weak to pip is not likely to survive.
2. If the shell is pipped but the chick does not start chipping a circle around the shell within 12 hours, use a pair of tweezers to gently break small pieces of shell from around the pip hole.
3. If you see blood, stop and wait a few hours. Otherwise, the chick will likely hemorrhage.
4. If the shell membrane dries out (changes from translucent white to parchment tan) gently moisten it. Do not drip water directly into the pip, or you run the risk of drowning the baby bird.
5. Above all, if you keep opening the incubator to see what's going on during the hatch, you contribute to the problem by reducing the humidity.

After the chicks hatch, leave them in the incubator for 12 to 24 hours, until they fluff out. The chicks will be wet when they hatch, and exposure to cold

Stages of chick development

9 Days

12 Days

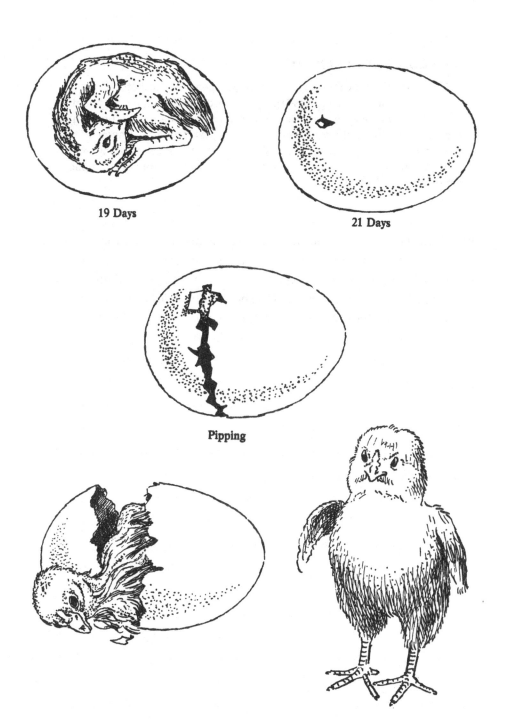

19 Days

21 Days

Pipping

air will chill them. When they have thoroughly dried, remove them to a ready and waiting brooder. During the first 24 to 48 hours, the chicks are still absorbing egg yolk and do not need to be fed, although giving them warm water right away reduces stress and the possibility of dehydration. Tips on raising your new chicks are offered in Chapter 10.

CARING FOR YOUR CHICKS

If we hadn't spent hours in our backyard watching baby chicks, we would never have realized how well-equipped for life baby birds are by comparison with babies of other animals. Sure, chicks need to be kept warm, and they need protection and a little help in finding food. But how remarkable is it that baby chicks walk and scamper about immediately upon hatching, and can fly within a week or so? From the moment they hatch, they can see, and they know how to eat; they can even understand a complete chicken vocabulary that includes cries of distress, the clucked expressions of motherly content-ment, and calls meaning "hawk–run" and "food–come." They fight, too, just like daddy roosters. In comparison, baby cats, rabbits, and people may be blind, helpless, mute, or immobile for several weeks or months.

SETTING UP A BROODER

When a hen does your hatching, she'll take care of the details of raising the chicks. But if you purchase chicks or hatch them in an incubator, all the joys of motherhood will be conferred onto you. Men will have to consent to be mothers, too, as baby chicks have little use for fathers.

To furnish all the same comforts that would be provided by a mother hen, you will need some sort of brooder in which to keep your chicks warm and safe while they grow. If you plan to raise a lot of chicks each year, you might find that a permanent brooder is a good investment. Brooders may be purchased from most of the same places that sell incubators and come in a variety of sizes and types, ranging from inexpensive kits to top-of-the-line metal outfits. A permanent brooder may be homemade once you know the principles involved.

If you plan on raising chicks once, or only a few each year, you can get by with a sturdy cardboard box for a brooder. Line the bottom with a thick layer of paper towels and partially cover the top with newspaper or cardboard to keep out drafts but still allow in some fresh air. The size of the box will depend on the size and number of chicks you intend to put in it, and it will have to be increased as the chicks grow. The chicks should have plenty of room to move around and to spread out to sleep. They should also have enough room to get away from the heat source when they want to.

The traditional way to provide brooder heat is to use a light bulb or an incandescent heat lamp in a spotlight reflector. Over the years, we've found that such lamps get too hot for brooding chicks in small numbers, and a bulb that falls can start a fire. For something more than an inexpensive but unsafe light bulb, an infrared radiant heat panel, such as Infratherm's Sweeter Heater, is a much safer choice. Such a panel is expensive, but it is energy efficient and lasts forever when properly cared for. It has the distinct advantage that it emits no light, and just like you do, your chicks will appreciate lights-out at bedtime. Once the chicks are grown, the heater panel may be used for other purposes, such as warming an injured or ill chicken or providing warmth over the coop roost on bitter winter nights.

If you choose to use a heater panel, you will need to provide some type of light 24/7 for the first 3 days, or until all the chicks are eating and drinking well. After that, you can turn the light out at night, which will allow the chicks to rest and also let them get used to the natural daily cycles of light and dark.

If you set up the brooder inside your house, you will soon learn that chicks produce an awful lot of fine dust that will settle on everything near and far, so you might want to confine the brooder to a spare room, bathroom, or closet with the door shut to keep the dust from spreading throughout the house. While raising our first brood of chicks, we had long-running family disputes over when the house was going to get cleaned, even if it had been only a half hour since the last dusting. Once the chicks were big enough to live outdoors, the problem disappeared, and the cause became apparent.

For the first 2 years we raised chicks, we put up with dust in the house. After we realized that chick-raising was going to be an ongoing activity, we purchased a proper brooder and installed it in the garage. But our friends persisted in remembering the earlier years, and for the longest time, we were known as the people with chickens in their living room. Visitors would enter our house, look around, and ask, "Don't you have chickens anymore?"

You might want to avoid the dust issue by setting up your brooder in a garage or other outbuilding with electricity, provided the place is draft-free, as well as predator- and kid-proof. If you have small children, explain to them that chicks, like human babies, need a lot of rest and can easily be loved to death by little hands squeezing them.

BROODING TEMPERATURE

The temperature in the brooder should start around 90°F for newly hatched chicks and be decreased by about 5°F each week until ambient temperature has been reached. You don't need a thermometer to regulate brooder heat. You'll be able to tell your chicks are happy by the sounds they make and by their body language. Happy chicks make contented, musical peeps. Chicks that are in distress from cold or hunger will tip you off with loud incessant cheeping.

Chicks that pant or press against the corners and edges of the box, away from the heat, are too hot and could possibly suffocate. Reduce bulb wattage,

 BROODER BEDDING

For the first couple of days, line the brooder floor with paper towels, which serves two purposes: to provide a nonslip surface while little chick legs are strengthening, and to prevent the chicks from eating litter until they learn to eat starter ration. Once the chicks are eating well, fine kiln-dried pine shavings make suitable brooder litter. Shredded paper works, too, although we find it tends to cling to the feet of feather-legged chicks more than shavings.

Chicks are susceptible to a number of chickhood diseases, so proper sanitation in the brooder is essential to keeping them healthy. Provide the box with fresh litter every couple of days. The litter should never be allowed to remain damp; if water is spilled, clean out and replace the wet litter.

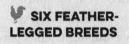

raise a heater panel, or get a bigger box. If the chicks huddle together in a pile under the heat, they are chilly. The heat source could be too high to be effective, bulb wattage could be too low, or the box could be too big and drafty. Cold chicks that huddle overnight or for any long period may smother each other.

Within comfortable limits, the more rapidly the brooder temperature is reduced, the more quickly the chicks will feather out. Comfortable chicks will pursue their normal activities of walking around, pecking at food, pecking at the sides of the box, drinking water, and sleeping, and sleeping, and sleeping. They need quite a lot of rest and will frequently lie about like a carpet on the brooder floor, with their heads down and wings spread out–a position that has alarmed more than a few people unfamiliar with the ways of chicks.

A friend once spent the night in our living room, where we had set up a small brooder. The chicks were active and lively when he went to sleep, but in the morning, they were all spread out motionless on the brooder floor. Our alarmed friend loudly announced that all the chicks had died in the night. Meanwhile, his commotion awakened the chicks. When we hurried to the living room to witness the death scene, our friend was confounded to see that the chicks had "come back to life" and were just as active as they had been the night before.

PROVIDING WATER

Chicks must have clean, fresh water available to them at all times. Inexpensive chick-drinkers are available from most poultry suppliers and feed stores. Their advantage is that they do not tip easily, and they have a small footprint, so they don't take up much brooder space. A nipple drinker is a popular option that is less apt to accumulate debris, dampen litter, or drown a chick.

Whatever type of water container you use, be sure the chicks cannot walk in it or fall into it. Chicks can drown from being mashed into the water dish by their brooder mates, and they will get droppings into the water if they can

walk in it. They may also get water on the litter and feed, causing unpleasant odors and unhealthful conditions.

When the chicks first arrive, have the drinker filled with warm water. The chicks may be slightly dehydrated if they arrived in the mail (see page 145) or were left in the incubator a little too long. As you place them into the brooder, gently dip each chick's beak into the water. The chicks will catch on rather quickly, and soon they all will be dipping their beaks in on their own.

FEEDING YOUR CHICKS

Chicks instinctively start pecking as soon as the opportunity arises. If you place a newly hatched chick on a sheet of newspaper, it will try to peck the print off the page. Once your chicks have started drinking, sprinkle chick starter crumbles on the paper towels lining the brooder floor. After they've pecked that up, put some starter in a clean tuna can, large jar lid, or cut-down tissue box. After a day or so, they will be ready to use a regular chick feeder, which may be purchased from any poultry supplier and most feed stores.

Chicks sometimes develop a condition called *pasting up*, also known as pasty butt, paste up, or sticky bottom. It happens when soft droppings stick to the vent area, build up, and harden. Eventually, the chick will no longer be able to poop, with dire consequences. Pasting may be caused by disease, but more often, it results from chilling, overheating, or improper feeding. A starter ration that's heavy on soybeans, for example, can trigger pasting.

If you see this condition starting, clean the chick's bottom right away. Wearing disposable gloves, gently moisten the hardened poop, then carefully pick off the mess with your fingers, taking care to minimize down removal and avoid tearing skin. Dry the chick's bottom, and apply a little petroleum jelly to prevent further pasting.

If several chicks in the brooder experience pasting, determining the cause may not be easy. One year, our chicks had a persistent pasting problem for no apparent reason, until we changed to a different brand of chick crumbles. The pasting problem immediately vanished, never to return.

Chicks should be fed a high-protein starter ration, which is usually available both with and without a medication that inhibits coccidiosis—a disease that is extremely common in chicks and can be deadly. The good news is that chicks gradually develop immunity to coccidiosis, which is therefore largely a concern mainly during early chickhood. To prevent coccidiosis, either have chicks vaccinated when purchased at a hatchery, or feed them a medicated starter.

The important word here is "or." If your chicks are vaccinated against coccidiosis, *do not* feed them medicated starter, as it will neutralize the vaccine.

If, however, your chicks have not been vaccinated, we strongly urge you as a first-time chicken-keeper to feed your chicks a medicated starter, according to the directions on the label. Once you have gained experience in raising chicks, you may choose to use nonmedicated starter in the future. For now, don't skew the learning curve and run the risk that your chicks will develop a deadly case of coccidiosis.

Other important measures in the prevention of coccidiosis include keeping brooder litter clean and dry and keeping feed free of droppings and moisture. Should your chicks manage to get water in their feed, replace it before it turns moldy. If damp feed becomes an ongoing problem, feed your chicks only a little at a time, but often.

Medicated crumbles may be discontinued with relative safety after about 8 weeks, as by then, your chicks will be building up a natural immunity to coccidiosis. Do continue with a high-protein feed so your chicks will grow well and remain healthy. As they reach maturity, gradually switch them over to an adult feeding program (see page 30).

GROWING UP

When your chicks are a week or two old, they can spend short periods outdoors on warm days. You might, for instance, sit with them on the lawn.

If you have too many chicks to keep an eye on, or you don't have time to watch over them, put them in a pen, such as the chicken tractor described on page 20. An enclosed pen will protect them from cats and other predators that might wander by and will keep the chicks from wandering away. The chicks will safely and happily scratch in the dirt or peck at weeds and bugs. Move the pen each day, so the chicks will have a fresh place in which to scratch. Be sure to provide shade so the chicks can get out of the hot sun when they want to, and hustle them back to their indoor brooder if rain threatens.

As the weather warms and the chicks grow protective plumage, they may be left in an outdoor pen for progressively longer periods but still should be brought in on chilly nights. When the weather has warmed sufficiently, and the chicks have most of their feathers (at 4 to 6 weeks), you can put them out permanently. We check on our chicks several times during their first few nights out, to make sure that they aren't huddling and smothering each other.

Chicks start thinking about perching as soon as their little wing feathers grow sufficiently to provide liftoff. Getting them into the habit of roosting early in their lives is a good idea, for at least two reasons. One is that, if you don't provide proper perches, they will roost on top of the feeder and drinker and poop in their feed and water. Another reason is that chicks that are not acquainted with a perch may have a hard time catching on once they're housed in a coop that's equipped with one. So start early by outfitting the brooder with small, low roosting bars. The adorable sight of those mini chickens roosting just like the grown-ups is sure to put a smile on your face.

PECKING-ORDER SQUABBLES

By the time they reach about 6 weeks of age, chicks begin jostling for position in the pecking order, a system of social organization designed to minimize tension and stress by ensuring that every member of a flock knows its place. All the cockerels will establish their order from the most authoritative on down to the meekest. All the pullets will do the same. Between the male hierarchy and the female hierarchy, the system becomes rather more complex.

In a flock of mixed genders and ages, generally, the older cocks will be at the top of the pecking order, then the older hens, then the young cockerels, and, finally, the young pullets. As the cockerels and pullets mature, they will work their way up the ladder among the hens, and the cockerel that reaches the top will then start trying to work his way in among the mature roosters. An aging rooster or hen may eventually lose its top-dog position to a more vigorous, young upstart.

Whenever you bring new chickens into your flock, the pecking order will reorganize as the newcomers jostle to find their place. They won't necessarily start at the bottom, and they are unlikely to find their way to the top any time soon.

INTEGRATING FLOCKS

If your coop already houses mature chickens when your growing chicks are ready to move in, don't summarily put them together, as the young ones will most likely get picked on. A better plan is to put the younger chickens into a roomy pen, coop, or cage inside or adjacent to the existing flock's coop or yard. The two groups can then get acquainted through the cage wire or fence, which the newbies can move away from, should things get dicey.

If you have few chickens and lots of space, a system that works nicely is to move the old flock to the separate coop or adjacent run and let the new ones into the main area, which they can then explore unhindered. When the two groups are eventually brought together, the newbies will be less intimidated than they would have been had they both encountered strange chickens and a strange environment at the same time. Adding extra feeding and drinking stations for the combined group also helps reduce territorial conflicts, which often center on access to food and water.

11

FINGER-LICKIN' BACKYARD CHICKEN

If the thought of eating chickens raised in your backyard makes you squeamish, feel free to skip this chapter. However, if you're looking forward to raising some of the best chicken you've ever had on your plate, read on. Chickens can put meat on your table faster and with less effort than any other livestock. In just a few weeks, your chicks reach target weight, your chicken-keeping chores are over, and your freezer is full of broilers that are tastier and better for you than anything you could buy at the store.

CHICKENS FOR MEAT

Some breeds are less suitable to raise for meat than others. Industrial-strength Leghorns, for example, will be tough and stringy by the time they grow enough meat to make a meal. On the other hand, even small bantams make tasty meat birds. We never hesitate to put our extra banty cockerels into the freezer. They're great whether roasted whole or simmered in a soup. In fact, we find that they give a soup or stew more flavor than any larger breed.

The fundamental difference among breeds raised specifically as broilers is the amount of time needed to grow the birds from hatch to harvest. The quicker they grow to target weight, the cheaper they are to raise and the more tender the meat. On the other hand, the longer they take, the more flavorful the meat. When growing chickens for the table, your basic choices are white Cornish hybrids, the industrial favorites; colored Cornish hybrids, preferred for free-ranging; and heritage or dual-purpose breeds, the choice of home-steaders who raise sustainable meat-and-egg flocks.

WHITE CORNISH HYBRIDS

The most efficient meat hybrids are an industrial creation developed by combining white Cornish and white Plymouth Rock genetics, and variously known as Cornish Rock, Cornish Game Hen, or Jumbo Cornish. These are the chickens you see cut and wrapped at the supermarket.

Their industrial-strength advantages are that they efficiently convert feed into meat, growing fast and being ready to harvest at 6 to 7 weeks of age. Chicks of the same sex and age grow at the same rate and therefore are ready to butcher at the same time. They are broad-breasted and produce a high percentage of tender white meat. The edible portion (excluding excess fat, intestines, feathers, head, feet, and blood) is about 75 percent of a bird's live weight.

They have white feathers, and fewer of them than most other breeds, making them fast and easy to pluck. And they have no underlying hairs to singe. We like them for roasting with the skin intact. When we raise other kinds of chickens for meat, we skin them.

The disadvantage of white Cornish hybrids as backyard chickens is that they do little more than eat. They don't like to travel far from the feeder, and their lack of exercise makes their meat soft and less tasty than that of more active breeds. Because of their excessively rapid growth, they must be butchered as soon as they reach target weight, before they become lame or die of heart failure.

COLORED CORNISH HYBRIDS

Colored Cornish hybrids are another industrial creation, developed for France's famous Label Rouge organic free-range chickens and adopted by America's pastured broiler industry. They grow less rapidly than white Cornish hybrids but faster than heavy pure breeds. They take at least 11 weeks to reach target weight, and even chicks of the same age and sex don't always grow at a uniform rate.

Per pound of meat produced, they eat about half again as much as white Cornish hybrids, partly because they take longer to grow and partly because they're better foragers, and the activity uses up calories that might otherwise go toward growth. But, because of their slower growth, their meat has more flavor. The edible portion is approximately 70 percent of live weight.

Most strains of colored Cornish hybrids have red feathers, but they may also be barred, black, gray, or any color but white. Their colored feathers make them less attractive to predators—a distinct advantage for free-range chickens—but they also make them more difficult to pluck clean.

SIX COLORED CORNISH HYBRIDS

Black Broiler

Freedom Ranger*

Kosher King

Redbro

Red Ranger

Silver Cross

*Gail's top pick

HERITAGE BREEDS

Many of us who keep a pure breed for eggs and periodically hatch some of the eggs to raise pullets as future layers invariably have plenty of extra cockerels to raise for meat. Many of the standard heritage breeds were developed precisely for this purpose, and they are good foragers.

However, they grow considerably slower than Cornish hybrids, requiring at least 16 weeks to reach target weight. They are not as efficient in converting feed into meat, and they don't grow at a uniform rate. That can be an advantage to those of us who don't care to engage in one long marathon plucking session.

Compared to Cornish crosses, these pure breeds have thinner breasts and more dark meat, with the edible portion being about 65 percent of live weight. Because they are more active, their meat is lower in fat, firmer in texture, and has a stronger chicken flavor.

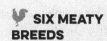

SIX MEATY BREEDS

Delaware

Jersey Giant

Naked Neck

New Hampshire*

Plymouth Rock

Wyandotte

*Gail's top pick

BROODING MEAT BIRDS

Brooding meat birds is similar to brooding other chickens, except that hybrids need more space because of their speedier growth rate and greater ultimate size. The white Cornish hybrids, in particular, eat almost constantly and drink a lot of water to wash down all that feed. The brooder, therefore, needs plenty of room to accommodate all that body mass, plus sufficient feeders and drinkers to go around.

The sheer size of white hybrid broilers keeps them warmer than other chickens of the same age. They tend to suffer in hot weather more than most other chickens. In a warm climate, they're best raised during the cooler days of spring or fall. White Cornish hybrids don't do well at temperatures much cooler than 65°F or much warmer than 85°F, while other chickens have a wider range of temperature tolerance.

Giving the chickens access to grass results in their meat containing less fat and more healthful omega-3s and other good nutrients. The activity of foraging creates darker, firmer, more flavorful meat, but also causes birds to eat more total ration because they take longer to reach target weight.

Some of the standard breeds retain the foraging instincts of their ancestors, so they take to grazing quite readily. By contrast, Cornish hybrids become pen potatoes unless they are introduced to foraging by 3 weeks of age; weather permitting, they may be moved outdoors as young as 2 weeks of age. The energy used for foraging slows their growth and makes them less susceptible to leg problems. The end result is a trade-off between faster growth versus better bird health and tastier meat.

FEEDING MEAT BIRDS

The main broiler management activity is to keep the feed and water coming. Broilers need fresh, clean water at all times to aid digestion and help prevent disease. Placing drinkers and feeders as far apart as possible encourages the birds to exercise and grow flavorful lean muscle rather than fat.

Most feed stores carry one all-purpose starter/grower ration (the same you would feed to any chicks), which may be used from start to finish. Some sources offer a range of rations with varying percentages of protein versus energy. More protein increases growth rate; more energy slows the growth rate and increases flavor. Some sources offer a full line of starter, grower, and finisher rations targeted to specific stages of broiler growth. When using these specialized feeds, follow directions on the label regarding when to switch from one ration to another, as each manufacturer's recommended schedule is based on the formulations of its particular rations.

The choices don't end there. Some sources offer certified organic, non-GMO, or soy-free rations. Some brands include a probiotic formula designed to stimulate the immune system and fend off disease. If the feed you use does not include probiotics, you may purchase them as a separate supplement from most poultry suppliers.

Medicated rations contain the drug amprolium to prevent coccidiosis, an intestinal disease that interferes with nutrient absorption and reduces growth rate. If your goal is to produce organic or naturally raised broilers, a nondrug alternative is to buy broiler chicks that have been vaccinated at the hatchery. A vaccine is not a drug; therefore, it may be used for organic or naturally raised chickens.

BUTCHERING AGE

The younger chickens are when they are butchered, the more tender the meat will be. On the other hand, chickens that are butchered too young will yield mushy, flavorless meat, and little of it. The older the chicken, the less efficient it becomes at converting feed into meat, the costlier it becomes to raise, and the firmer the meat becomes, to the point of toughness. After you raise broilers for a time, you'll figure out the age at which they taste best to you and your family.

White Cornish hybrids are generally ready to harvest at about 6 weeks of age, at which time they make good fryers. We prefer to roast them whole when they are larger, so we raise them until they are 8 weeks of age. That age also represents the point of diminishing returns, when the birds consume more feed while putting on less weight. At 8 weeks of age, our Cornish roasters have hardly any fat.

The earliest you would want to harvest colored Cornish hybrids is about 9 weeks of age, although most people prefer them at 11 weeks, or even older.

Their slower growth is due partially to genetics and partially to their greater degree of activity.

Most of the chickens we serve at our house are products of our own breeding programs. We hatch chicks from our own chickens and butcher the surplus cockerels and less-than-ideal pullets. In other words, we follow the old-time philosophy: Breed the best, eat the rest (otherwise known as culling). Over the decades, we have continued this practice with flocks of New Hampshires, Plymouth Rocks, Orpingtons, Rhode Island Reds, Welsumers, and a variety of bantam breeds.

Generally, we start in on the cockerels at 8 to 10 weeks of age, about the time they begin to crow. Some may be a little on the small side, but by the time we've worked through all the unwanted cockerels, they're getting a little on the too-large side. By the age of 16 weeks–the generally recommended age for butchering purebreds for meat–they are putting on more fat than we like to see. Excess fat is an indication of wasted feed, and we want our feed dollars to go into edible muscle, not fat.

Nevertheless, a purebred meat breed is still fairly tender until about 22 weeks. Any chicken that grows old and tough is relegated to the slow-cooker.

🐓 EASY WAYS OUT

If you want to raise chickens for meat but don't care to do the butchering yourself, you might find a poultry slaughtering service through the yellow pages of your phone book, the classified section of your local newspaper, or your county's Cooperative Extension office. Check with the service well in advance regarding their prices and specific procedures. You may need to find such a service if local regulations bar you from butchering chickens in your own yard.

Even assuming that you don't mind doing the job yourself, once you've plucked a few chickens, you may wish you had a mechanical chicken plucker, which can do the job in mere seconds. You might find someone local willing to loan out or rent you a plucker. A good mechanical plucker is expensive, but it is a real time-saver if you intend to do a lot of butchering. For occasional plucking, a feather removal drill attachment can be a helpful device.

After we spent many years plucking chickens, only to remove the skin when we cooked the meat, we finally came to the realization that skinning a chicken in the first place is a lot faster than plucking. Now the only chickens we pluck are the ones we plan to roast whole for holiday occasions.

After tough meat has stewed for about 12 hours in a slow-cooker, it becomes falling-off-the-bone tender. We pick out the bones and stir in a jar of barbecue sauce. Heavenly!

If you're in doubt about the age of the chicken you plan to butcher, check the breastbone—the more flexible the breastbone, the more tender the meat will be.

Not incidentally, you'll find that homegrown chicken meat is darker in color than you might be used to, because of the birds' greater level of activity compared to industrially produced chickens. In bantams that fly, even the breast meat tends to be dark.

An important criterion in deciding when to butcher is whether or not the chickens are molting. If they are in the middle of a molt, plucking will be much more difficult than it would be after the feathers fully emerge. If you find yourself butchering chickens that are molting, skin them.

Assuming that you have determined the time is right, in preparation for butchering day, remove the chickens' feed overnight to give their digestive tracts time to empty. Leave the water, however, so the chickens won't get dehydrated.

HOW TO KILL A CHICKEN

The most important thing about killing a chicken is to do it swiftly and humanely. No matter how many times you do it, killing a chicken is never fun. A dead chicken reflexively flaps its wings and pumps its legs. If you let go of the chicken, it will thrash wildly on the ground for several minutes. Don't worry, it won't really run around with its head cut off, as the proverb says.

The traditional way to kill a chicken is to hold the chicken by the legs, lay its head on a chopping block, and chop off the head with a good, sharp ax. A problem with this method is that the chicken reflexively twists its neck around, splattering blood.

A less messy way is to take hold of the chicken's legs and head, and stretch its neck until you feel the skull slip away from the neck, a method technically known as cervical dislocation. As the neck joint slips, the spinal cord and blood vessels break, resulting in rapid death, as well as natural bleeding out. Bleeding is essential to preserving the meat's flavor, appearance, and keeping quality.

HOW TO PLUCK A CHICKEN

The best time we've ever made plucking chickens is about 15 minutes per bird. We typically do four chickens at a time, which takes about an hour. Then, if we're still in the mood, we go back for four more.

Have a large kettle or canning pot of water heating on the stove or, better yet, on an outdoor burner. The ideal temperature is between 120° F and 160°F. Water that's allowed to come to a full boil will cook the skin and cause it to tear when you start pulling out feathers. The pot should be only about three-quarters full of water. When you add the chicken, the water level will rise, and you don't want hot water spilling out onto the burner.

Dip one chicken at a time into the hot water, holding it by the feet and using the stiff legs to push it under (you'll see how this works the first time you try it). Avoid scalding your hand while moving the chicken around in the water for about 30 seconds, which opens the pores so the feathers will release easily. Pull the chicken out of the water and lay it in a sink or on a table, taking care not to drip hot water down your front or on your bare feet (you can guess how we figured this out).

Then start stripping off the feathers as fast as you can, pulling them in the direction they grow so the skin doesn't tear. The reason for not tearing the skin is purely aesthetic, so if that happens, don't panic and throw the chicken out–instead, smother it in mushrooms.

If the feathers don't come off easily, either the water wasn't hot enough or you didn't leave the bird in the water long enough, so do it again. After a while, you'll know how long to dip it. If plucking hot feathers burns your fingers, run cold tap water over the bird to cool it down.

We like to pluck the wings first, because as the bird stiffens, cleaning the feathers out from its wingpits becomes more difficult. After the feathers have been removed, tweeze the small pinfeathers using a paring knife and your thumb. When you get one chicken done, rinse off any loose feathers that may be sticking, pat with a paper towel to start it drying, set it aside, and go on to the next.

Unless you are plucking white Cornish hybrids, you'll need to singe off the hairlike things that stick up after the bird has dried a bit. The reason you don't need to singe industrial-strength broilers is that the wise breeders have genetically removed these hairs. Any other chicken must be passed over a flame to burn off the hairs. Not too close; you don't want to roast the chicken yet. The flame might be provided by a gas burner, a propane torch, or, if you want to get fancy, a poultry singeing torch, which looks remarkably like a handyman's propane torch.

HOW TO GUT A CHICKEN

Once the feathers have been removed, gut the chicken. Cut off the legs where the shank joins the drumstick. Then, cut the stub of the neck back to clean meat. Cut off the little bump on the tail, making sure to get all the yellow stuff around it, too. This bump is the oil gland, and the yellow stuff is oil used by chickens to shine up their feathers. People have told us it tastes terrible. We'll take their word for it.

With the chicken on its back and using a small, sharp knife, make an incision just forward of the vent, and slit through the skin. We typically slit from the vent to the breastbone, but if you plan to stuff the chicken for roasting, a sideways slit better keeps the skin over the breast. Either way, don't cut deep, as you don't want to puncture the intestine.

Then, loosen the organs by entering through this slit, work your hand all around the inside cavity of the bird between the body wall and the organs. When you feel the organs have loosened, reach in as far as you can, and pull the innards gently toward you. If you're lucky, almost everything will come out in one neat bundle.

Cut around the vent to release the organs completely, and separate out the gizzard, liver, and heart, if you want to save them.

Cleaning the gizzard is a little tricky if you've never seen one whole. The

Cutting out the oil gland

gizzard is roundish and closed up something like a clam around an inner sac. The sac has a tough lining and is filled with little stones and sometimes glass chips, tacks, and other weird stuff. Slice the gizzard halfway around and take out the inside lining. If you do a good job slicing through the outer part (the part you want to save), you won't cut into the inner sac, and it will just peel away with the odds and ends still inside. But, if you happen to cut all the way through, just rinse out the flotsam before peeling away the lining. We are not overly fond of heart and gizzard meat, per se, but we find that, after it's been run through a meat grinder, it makes terrific pizzas and tacos.

The liver needs some cleaning, too. It has a little green bile sac attached to it. Cut it off, taking great care not to break it, or the liver will taste bitter. Once bile contaminates a liver, it won't rinse off. Chicken livers (sans bile) are a tasty treat, so save them up and do something spectacular with them. Our favorite butchering-day dinner is quick-fried chopped liver piled on a loaded potato with cheddar cheese and bacon bits. Pass the ranch dressing, please.

Sometimes, the heart will be left way up inside the cavity. If so, reach in and pull it out. Remove the lungs, too; they are the spongelike pink things clinging between the ribs. If you're doing a rooster, remove the testicles, which are two white oval objects about in the middle of the back. If it's a hen, you may find a cluster of tiny egg yolks along the backbone. You may even find a whole egg, shell and all, in the bundle of innards.

Then turn the bird on its breast and slit the neck skin a few inches toward the body. Pull out the windpipe and the crop, if they didn't come out with the other organs, and cut off the neck. Wash the chicken thoroughly in cold running water inside and out, drain, pat dry–and you're done!

By now, you will have recognized the chicken as much like a whole

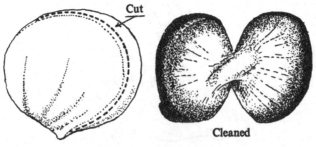

Cutting the gizzard

chicken you'd buy at the market. If you want to cut it into pieces, you should have a pretty good idea how to proceed. For reassurance, you can find any number of websites depicting in graphic detail how to cut up a whole chicken.

STORING CHICKEN MEAT

Chicken meat must be aged in the refrigerator for 24 to 48 hours so rigor mortis can run its course, after which the meat will soften up again. If you don't allow this aging period, the meat will be a little tough. Whether you age the chickens whole or cut into pieces makes no difference.

After the chickens have aged, you can either cook them or store them in the freezer. We find that double-wrapped chicken stored in a freezer that maintains a temperature of –10°F will keep well for a year. To double-wrap a whole chicken, first seal it in a plastic bag and then in a second plastic bag. To double-wrap pieces, first wrap them tightly in plastic wrap, then in butcher paper. Double-wrapping reduces the development of ice crystals and freezer burn. If you use a vacuum sealer, double-wrapping isn't necessary.

BUTCHERING BOTTOM LINE

We're often asked if raising backyard broilers will save you money. Sorry, but no. For one thing, feed isn't cheap. For another, you can't expect to compete with the efficiency of the chicken industry with a small flock roaming your

backyard. But you will know exactly what your chickens have been fed and how they have been processed. And you will notice the flavor advantage of growing your chickens to an older age that cannot be matched by a mass-production operation.

You will find that butchering chickens gives you a whole new appreciation for the meat you eat. Remember, all that meat hermetically sealed in pristine plastic packages at the supermarket was once living animals, and somewhere, somebody is making a living spilling their blood all day long. You'll have to come to terms with this fact on your own. We have plenty of friends who butchered chickens one day and became vegetarians the next.

SHOWING YOUR CHICKENS

Raising standard-bred chickens for show can be an interesting and rewarding hobby. If you go into it without preparation, however, the fun can easily turn into frustration. In this brief chapter, we hope to convince you that showing and breeding for show are not as simple as bundling up a pet chicken and trundling off to a competition. Before deciding to exhibit your chickens, visit a few poultry shows, join one or more local or national poultry organizations, and, above all, look, listen, and ask loads of questions to gain an understanding of the subtleties and intricacies involved.

GETTING UP TO SPEED

A good way to enter the world of exhibition poultry is by joining a local or statewide poultry fanciers club. By attending local meetings, you will connect with other people who are interested in showing chickens. They can help you get started by telling you where you might obtain good show stock and by answering your questions on the unique care show birds need.

If you already know what breed you want to show, join a national organization that specializes in that breed. Most of them have websites offering pertinent information about their chosen breed and listing members who raise and sell show-quality birds.

An indispensable resource is a copy of the *American Standard of*

Perfection, published by the American Poultry Association (APA). The *Standard* includes descriptions of all the APA-recognized breeds, with illustrations to acquaint you with what they should look like. The birds you will want for show should look as much as possible like the ones described in the *Standard.*

If your chosen show bird is a bantam, also obtain the *Bantam Standard,* published by the American Bantam Association (ABA). Although the APA *Standard* does include bantams, the breed and variety descriptions are not always identical to those in the *Bantam Standard.* Once you get your feet wet, membership in the APA and/or the ABA makes you eligible for prizes offered at their respective sanctioned shows.

For serious exhibitors, a subscription to the monthly newspaper *Poultry Press* (or, in Canada, *Feather Fancier*) is a must-have. Each issue announces dates and contact information for upcoming shows around the country, reports on the winners of past competitions, often contains useful articles about breeding and caring for show chickens, and includes ads for just about anything you might want or need related to exhibiting your chickens.

CHICKENS FOR SHOW

The best way to find out what show chickens look like is to attend exhibitions and see the real deal for yourself. Try to determine why the judges ranked the birds as they did. Compare the winning birds with those placing second and third, and compare them all with the pictures in the *Standard.*

Always take the *Standard* along when you intend to look at show chickens. Many well-respected show judges carry a *Standard* while judging exhibitions, and they consult it before making any important decisions, despite having judged chickens for so long that they likely have the entire book memorized.

By first acquainting yourself with birds at competitions, you will be better able to make wise choices in purchasing your own stock. Once you are ready to purchase show chickens, exercise caution in deciding whom to buy them from. Many people raise and sell pet-quality purebreds. While these chickens roughly fit the description of their breeds and are readily identifiable as such, they are not likely to win any prizes.

"Not likely" doesn't mean never. We know one fellow who bought a chick at the local farm store, raised it to maturity, entered it in the county fair, and walked away with first prize. But, that was beginner's luck more than skill and is certainly not a good formula for raising consistent winners.

BUY OR BREED

A big temptation for beginning exhibitors is to go out and buy the best chicken they can afford, enter it into shows, and enjoy the pride of winning first place time after time. Whatever skill is involved in grooming a chicken that someone else bred, the real skill is in breeding your own show stock.

Chicken-keepers who've been seriously bitten by the show bug invariably want to breed their own potential prizewinners. The reason is that no chicken looks exactly like its description in the *Standard*, and serious exhibitors develop breeding strategies to raise birds that come as close as possible to the ideal for their breed. After a few years, each breeder's flock has an unmistakable look. Show judges and fellow exhibitors can identify these breeders just by looking at one of their chickens.

We have several friends who breed particularly outstanding show chickens and have rooms full of trophies attesting to the quality of their birds. Invariably, along comes a newbie who aspires to win big at show and, wishing to take a shortcut, offers an obscene amount of money for a top winner, and then proceeds to best everyone, including the bird's original owner. We once asked a breeder how he felt about being beaten by someone who had bought the winning bird from him. He replied that it made him feel good, because he knew he had bred the bird, and so did everyone else.

When buying chickens for show or as show-breeder stock, look not only at the bird you intend to purchase but also, if possible, at its parents, siblings, and offspring to determine if they are of consistent quality. A good seller will be happy to help you make a decision, pointing out any problems each bird may have, as well as its finer qualities. And be prepared for sticker shock when you hear the price; a show-quality chicken sells for many times more than your run-of-the-mill backyard chicken.

A common newbie mistake is to want to enter

SIX POPULAR BANTAMS FOR EXHIBITION

Cochin

Modern Game

Old English Game

Plymouth Rock

Silkie

Wyandotte

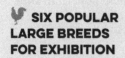

SIX POPULAR LARGE BREEDS FOR EXHIBITION

Australorp

Brahma

Cochin

Jersey Giant

Plymouth Rock

Rhode Island Red

many different breeds into competition, with the hope that at least some will come out winners. A better strategy is to select a breed and variety to specialize in. Once you get good at that, you will be ready to expand into different varieties of the same breed, or into a different breed altogether.

Electing to specialize in a popular show breed has both advantages and disadvantages. The advantage is that good show-quality stock is more readily available. The disadvantage is that competition will be stiffer. The rarer breeds have fewer competitors, but finding show-quality birds is more difficult, and so is finding a judge with experience in evaluating the breed.

Choosing a breed and obtaining good-quality stock is just the beginning for someone who is serious about raising birds for show. Show birds require specialized housing arrangements, a feeding program aimed at keeping the birds in peak condition, and a more carefully regulated breeding program than is necessary for the average backyard chickens. They also require specific attention before and after each show.

THE PREMIUM LIST

An excellent way to prepare yourself for showing chickens is to obtain a copy of the premium list before you attend a show, even if you are not yet ready to show your own chickens. The premium list tells you when and where the show will be held, which organizations, if any, have sanctioned the show, fees exhibitors are required to pay, the deadline for registering to enter the show, and what prizes are offered.

Prizes are also called *premiums*, which is how the premium list got its name, and typically include ribbons, trophies, and small amounts of cash. Most people spend more money preparing for and entering shows than they win back in prizes, although top contenders do sometimes come out ahead, or at least break even.

The premium list also includes the rules for entering—such as any required vaccinations, blood tests, or health certificates—and the specific

SHOW CLASSES: LARGE BREEDS

American: Buckeye, Chantecler, Delaware, Dominique, Holland, Java, Jersey Giant, Lamona, New Hampshire, Plymouth Rock, Rhode Island Red, Rhode Island White, Wyandotte

Asiatic: Brahma, Cochin, Langshan

English: Australorp, Cornish, Dorking, Orpington, Redcap, Sussex

Continental: Barnevelder, Campine, Crèvecoeur, Faverolle, Hamburg, Houdan, La Fleche, Lakenvelder, Polish, Welsumer

Mediterranean: Andalusian, Ancona, Catalana, Leghorn, Minorca, Sicilian Buttercup, Spanish

Other: Ameraucana, Araucana, Aseel, Cubalaya, Frizzle, Malay, Modern Game, Naked Neck, Old English Game, Phoenix, Shamo, Sultan, Sumatra, Yokohama

requirements for each class. A class is a group of similar chickens judged against each other, organized according to *Standard* classifications. Not all shows accept chickens in all classifications. Each chicken entered into a show must be registered in one of the classes named in the premium list. Entering a chicken in the wrong class is embarrassing–the entry will be marked "out of class" and will not be judged, so you might as well have left the bird at home and saved yourself the entry fee.

Each bird must also be correctly entered according to its breed and variety, and whether it is a cock, hen, cockerel, or pullet. A cock is a mature male chicken, at least 1 year old. A cockerel is a male chicken under 1 year of age. Similarly, a hen is a female chicken, at least 1 year old, while a pullet is a female chicken under 1 year of age.

Having a copy of the premium list with you the first few times you attend a show will help you sort out the details and avoid confusion when you finally feel ready to show your own chickens. If anything in the premium list seems not to make sense to you, most of the exhibitors you meet at the show will be happy to demonstrate how smart they are by explaining things to you.

At each poultry show, you will meet some highly competitive people for whom winning is everything. You will also meet a lot of people who rarely win, if at all, but continue to show their chickens for the joy of being with other people who share their interest in all things chicken.

SHOW PREP

Assuming you feel ready to dive in, well before show time, separate the males from the females and the males from each other. Injuries occur when males fight with one another or mate with the females. Separating your show specimens prevents further injuries and allows time for any existing injuries to heal.

Examine each bird to make sure it is healthy, free of lice and mites, and has no other disqualifications. The *Standard* lists all the possible reasons for a chicken to be disqualified. Some disqualifications apply to specific breeds, others apply to all chickens. General disqualifications include a crooked back, a wry or crooked tail, and stubs (downy feathers on the shanks or toes of a clean-legged breed). Such features are disqualifications because they are nearly always passed on to the offspring.

After deciding which of your birds are acceptable to show, you next need to spend time conditioning and training them. Conditioning involves feeding and grooming each chicken to look its best, including giving the bird a bath. Numerous websites offer step-by-step instructions for washing a chicken prior to an exhibition.

Training involves teaching each bird how to act while on display, and preparing it for the experience of being judged. An unprepared bird is likely to be frightened. It may crouch in the show cage and attempt to fly when anyone comes near. It may struggle when the judge handles it, making the judge's job more difficult. A calm, well-trained chicken nearly always places higher than an unprepared frightened bird.

However, chickens, like judges, have their good days and bad days. A bird may display itself differently from one day to the next, because of changes in its physical condition, health, training, or stress level. Even the fairest judge may place the same group of birds in one order on one day and in a different order on another day. If a bird doesn't place high in its class, don't be hasty to cull it until you find out why the bird did poorly. The best bird in the world won't win if it lacks maturity, is out of condition, or is out of sorts on the day of the show.

HOW THE JUDGING WORKS

At most shows, the judges look at birds individually in their coops. The ones with the best conformation, or body type, are usually removed from the coop and examined more closely. Most judges prefer to concentrate on their job without interruption. During the judging, spectators may be barred from the showroom, or at least from the area where the judge is working. But afterward, most judges are willing to discuss the placings.

Within each classification, the entries are organized according to breed, then variety, then gender. The judge starts by examining all the birds of one variety, gender, and age, then moves on to the next gender and age within the same variety. After all four groups (cock, hen, cockerel, pullet) within one variety have been judged, the winners within each group are compared with one another, and the best specimen of that variety is chosen as Best of Variety. The second best is designated Reserve of Variety.

The judge then moves on to the next variety within the same breed, and follows the same procedure in selecting Best of Variety and Reserve of Variety. After all the varieties within a breed have been judged, the winners within each variety are compared and the Best of Breed is selected. The second best is Reserve of Breed.

When all the breeds within a class have been judged, the winners for each breed are compared and the Class Champion is chosen. The runner-up becomes Reserve Class Champion. At this point, the showroom starts to buzz with excitement, because all the Class Champions and Reserve Champions are moved to Champion Row.

The champion large breeds will be compared to one another, and a Champion Large Fowl will be selected, as well as a Reserve Champion Large Fowl. Then all the champion bantams will be compared, and a Champion Bantam and Reserve Champion Bantam will be chosen. If the show includes other types of poultry, such as turkeys, ducks, or geese, the same procedures will apply to them.

And finally, all the champions are compared to one another, and the Grand Champion of Show and Reserve Grand Champion are announced. At this point, showroom tension is typically released in either cheers or tears.

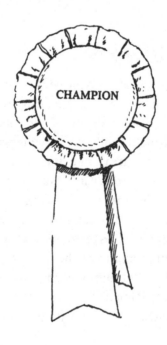

AFTER THE SHOW

Each time you return home from a show, clean and disinfect all carriers, waterers, feeders, and other equipment you took to the show. Isolate your returning birds for at least 2 weeks, and watch for any sign of disease. To avoid the possibility of infecting your chickens that stayed at home, continue to feed them first before caring for the returning show birds. Despite these necessary precautions, take heart in knowing that most people who raise chickens for show take great pride in the good health of their potential winners and would not knowingly show a chicken that might spread a contagious disease.

TIPS AND TRICKS FOR HAPPY, HEALTHY CHICKENS

Based on some of the poultry forums we see online, many first-time chicken-keepers appear to be scared witless by warnings about things that can go wrong. But rest assured that if you provide your flock with a clean and healthy environment, a nutritionally balanced diet, abundant fresh water, and plenty of loving care, major problems are unlikely to arise. The tips described in this chapter are offered to help further smooth the way toward making your chicken-raising venture easy and enjoyable.

CATCHING A CHICKEN

A handy thing to know is how to catch a chicken, which is fairly easy–once you're onto chicken psychology. If it fits into your plans, the best way to catch a chicken is at night after the flock has gone to roost. They will be asleep when you come in, and you can easily pick one right off the perch.

On the other hand, if you have raised your chickens as pets, and they are used to being handled, simply reach down and pick one up anytime during the day. Having calm, friendly chickens is one excellent reason for being on familiar terms with every bird in your flock.

To catch a less-friendly chicken, corner it in the coop or against a fence and grab it either by the legs or by clamping down on both wings. If you miss the first time, the chicken will become wilier and more difficult to corner.

For catching an intractable chicken, a long-handled net is ideal. It looks like a fishnet, and, in fact, if you already have a fishnet, it'll work fine for the purpose. Throw down some scratch to attract the bird's attention and distract it while you sneak up with the net.

Whatever your method, move rapidly but deliberately, rather than run or lunge suddenly. A frightened chicken may fly up into the rafters, into a tree, or over the fence. Having a helper to run interference can make things easier. On the other hand, someone who is unfamiliar with the ways of chickens can be worse than useless. We usually advise such well-meaning visitors to please stand out of the way.

A neighbor once told us we could have all her banties, if we could catch them. Confident that we would have no trouble, we went over only to find them running loose in a large backyard. Even though we had brought along two friends, the bantams were so wild that we succeeded only in scattering them into the trees, into the vacant lot next door, and under the neighbor's house. We suspect that someone had attempted to catch those chickens previously, causing them to become leery of further attempts to be caught. The trick to catching a chicken is to get it right the first time.

WING-CLIPPING

Some breeds, and especially bantam breeds, typically like to fly. Others might tend to fly while they're growing but then settle down after they mature.

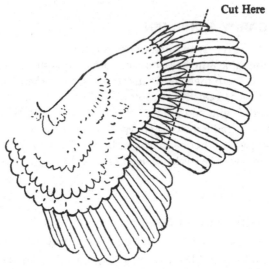

Where to clip the wing

Chickens that fly out of their yards can be a nuisance, as well as exposing themselves to predators.

If you have chickens that like to fly about and get themselves into trouble, and covering their run is not an option, you might want to ground them by clipping their wings. Wing-clipping is easily done by using a pair of sharp shears. Cut back the end one-third of the flight feathers of only one wing. The feathers will grow back after a molt, so you may eventually need to reclip them.

Wing-clipping does not harm a chicken, although to hear some of them squawk, you might think it was killing them. The idea behind wing-clipping is to upset the bird's balance enough that it can't lift itself far off the ground.

Wing-clipping has a few disadvantages. It does somewhat spoil the bird's appearance, which bothers some chicken-keepers. If you expect to show the bird, it will be disqualified if the feathers don't grow back before the show. Also, chickens with clipped wings that forage in a pasture or orchard may have difficulty escaping a predator.

PREDATORS

Once upon a time, a female cat lived in the field behind our house. Each spring, she would slip over our fence to find food for her latest litter of kittens, and our little chicks disappeared one by one. If you have a mysterious marauder pillaging your flock, you might set a live trap to catch it. That way, if the midnight skulker turns out to be your neighbor's pet, you will not only have positive proof who the offender is but also you may be able to avoid a possible feud by returning the animal unharmed.

The culprit might be anything from a weasel or skunk to a fox or raccoon, which means you may need professional help or at least a depredation permit. In many areas, to trap animals legally, you need a permit, which will be issued only if you can prove that you have diligently attempted all other means of excluding predators from your poultry yard. This concept is important, because it means that you bear the ultimate responsibility for providing secure fences and housing to keep your chickens safe from predators.

Dogs roaming loose are by far the most common poultry predator. Should you ever have an issue with a neighbor's dog, be aware of your legal rights. Laws vary with the locale, but nowhere need you put up with a dog marauding chickens in your own yard. Hopefully, you can settle the matter amicably with your neighbor. If not, and the problem persists, you might want to prosecute the uncooperative owner for recovery of your loss.

Some areas have pretty stiff laws covering such eventualities. A fellow we know, for instance, raises awesome show bantams. The neighbor's dog broke in and killed one of his chickens. The neighbor was uncooperative

CONTROLLING RODENTS

Sooner or later, you will almost certainly have an infestation of rats or mice in your coop, robbing the chicken's rations. Rodents tend to move indoors during fall and winter, when they seek food and shelter. Rats eat eggs and chicks, and both rats and mice can consume copious amounts of chicken feed.

Discourage rodents by eliminating piles of wood, scrap, unused equipment, and all other potential hiding places. Store feed in containers with tight-fitting lids, and immediately sweep up any spills. Remove feed from the coop at night, and place the feeder where rodents can't get to it. Rats need lots of water, so if the drinker is removed overnight, that measure alone may be sufficient to encourage rats to vacate.

Trapping is an option, but all traps are messy to deal with. Consider poisoning as a last resort. You might end up poisoning a pet, a child, or innocent wildlife. Besides, poison works best when rodents can't find anything else to eat, and when that's the case, they will leave on their own anyway.

about controlling his dog, so our friend took the neighbor to court. The law in his area provided for compensation in the amount of double damages. As luck would have it, our friend could prove he had recently sold one of his show birds for $100. The dog owner ended up paying court costs plus $200 for the dead chicken. You can bet that ended the dog's chicken-killing adventures.

 SIX HEAT-TOLERANT BREEDS

Andalusian

Fayoumi*

Leghorn

Naked Neck*

Polish

Sultan

*Gail's top picks

HOT WEATHER

During hot summer days, chickens stand around in the shade with their wings held away from their bodies, panting through wide-open beaks. Chickens cannot tolerate extreme heat and can easily die from heat stress. Since chickens don't perspire, air circulation and lots of drinking water are their methods of keeping cool.

An ample supply of cool drinking water is especially important in hot weather. As water circulates through the chicken's digestive system, it picks up body heat, helping cool the chicken down. Chickens, therefore, drink much more than usual during hot weather, and, as a result, their poop becomes moister. But they won't drink sufficient amounts if the water is warm. Keep drinkers in the shade, and refresh them often. If you can't be there to frequently provide cool water, place chunks of ice in the drinker. Plastic soda bottles filled two-thirds to three-quarters with water, and kept in the freezer, are handy reusable cool-water devices.

When the temperature is extremely high but humidity is low, spray the yard and coop roof with a hose or set a sprinkler out to create cooling through evaporation. On exceptionally hot and dry days, we sometimes spray the chickens with a fine mist. Above all, make sure they have a shady place in which to loll, and lots of space so they can spread away from each other to enjoy good air circulation.

FROSTBITTEN COMBS

In colder climates, frostbite is potentially a hazard to chickens during freezing weather, especially where conditions are damp and drafty. Particularly vulnerable are large combs and dangly wattles. Frostbite is less likely to affect breeds with tight-fitting combs.

The first sign of a frostbitten comb is a tip that appears pale, gray, or white. Swelling follows, then blistering, and finally the affected part may eventually die back and fall off. If you suspect that a chicken has been frostbitten, thaw the comb by carefully applying a warm, damp cloth for 15 minutes, rewarming the cloth, as needed. Do not directly apply heat (such as from a hair dryer or heating pad), which would increase the pain, and do not rub the affected area, which would increase the damage. After the comb has thawed, gently apply a hydrogel wound spray, such as Vetericyn, to promote healing and protect the comb from infection.

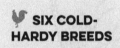

SIX COLD-HARDY BREEDS

Australorp

Buckeye*

Chantecler*

Delaware

Orpington

Wyandotte

*Gail's top picks

Frostbitten combs and wattles are extremely painful once they have thawed. The bird may become listless and stop eating. Isolate such a bird and provide a feeder and drinker of a type that won't rub against the comb and cause further pain. Although pet bowls are generally not the best feeders and drinkers for chickens, in this case, they are a good option. If infection sets in, amputation of the comb and wattles may be necessary.

Controlling coop humidity is an important frostbite-prevention measure. During winter, when chickens tend to spend more time inside the coop, moisture released by both droppings and respiration can easily become excessive. If the inside of the coop window drips with moisture, improve the ventilation.

Providing a flat-panel heater where chickens can opt to roost beneath it, or not, is a helpful measure, although heating the entire coop is a decidedly bad idea. Chickens adapt to weather as the seasons change, and providing heat for full-grown chickens will only confuse their metabolisms and make them even more vulnerable to the cold.

LEG BANDS

A handy way to keep track of such things as a chicken's age or where it came from is to apply a numbered or color-coded leg band around the chicken's shank. Bands may be purchased from suppliers of general poultry equipment and come in several sizes for different size chickens.

If you band your chickens, watch to make sure that the shank doesn't expand around the band, which will cause swelling, infection, and lameness. When bands are applied to young birds, take care to increase the band size as the birds grow.

FEATHER LOSS

First-time chicken-keepers are sometimes alarmed by the molt, when chickens lose their feathers and get new ones, which usually occurs each autumn.

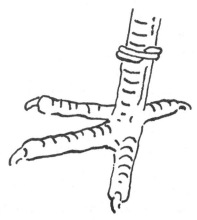

Expandable banding spiral

It doesn't happen to all the chickens at once, and, most of the time, it happens so gradually, it's hardly noticeable. But, sometimes, a chicken may look almost bare naked. You can tell a molt has started when your chicken yard suddenly seems to be littered with feathers. During the molt, make sure your birds are getting a proper diet, with plenty of protein to help their bodies build new feathers. Chickens that appear to be going through a hard molt–as indicated by a major loss of feathers all at the same time–can benefit from a molting supplement, available at pet shops for caged birds.

Feather loss occurring in the spring in the form of bare patches across a hen's back or on her head occurs when a rooster holds on with his claws and beak during breeding, as described on page 45. Once the feathers have been rubbed off a hen's back, the cock may claw through the skin, causing serious wounds. As soon as you notice a hen's feathers are missing, either isolate the hen, remove the rooster, or outfit the hen with a breeding saddle.

Another cause of feather loss is a type of mite, appropriately known as the depluming mite, which burrows into the chicken's skin. To relieve the irritation, the chicken scratches and picks at its feathers, and sometimes pulls them out. To prevent this cause of feather loss, keep the coop clean and mite-free, as described in "Mites and Lice" (page 129).

Feather loss may also result from picking, or the pulling out of one chicken's feathers by another chicken. Feather picking is typically the first sign of cannibalism.

CANNIBALISM

Yikes! It sounds scary, but bored or overcrowded chickens sometimes resort to cannibalism as an interesting diversion. This bad habit most commonly involves young birds, often because they are too crowded, too hot, or subjected to bright lights 24/7. Nutritional deficiencies or inadequate watering and feeding space may be contributing factors, as is brooding chicks on hardware cloth rather than on a solid floor.

Bored chicks often start by picking each other's toes, or even their own. Brooded chicks may enjoy having a toy of some sort to play with. For instance, they like to peck at shiny objects hanging from the ceiling or attached to the wall, such as an aluminum pie tin or an acrylic mirror. They also enjoy reaching for and eating suspended leafy greens, which might be enclosed in a hanging treat ball designed for this purpose.

Preventing overcrowding is essential. Chicks grow with astonishing rapidity–just like popcorn. So plan ahead. Increase the size of the available space as the chicks grow. Also, feed them a high-protein diet suitable for their age. And once they are eating and drinking well, dim the lights or, better yet, provide a heat source other than a light bulb so you can turn off the lights altogether at night. For providing brooder heat, a flat-panel radiant heater is ideal.

If cannibalism appears to be starting in the brooder, replace the light source with a red bulb and keep the brooder away from direct sunlight. A red light neutralizes the red color of blood, making it less attractive. A variety of antipicking preparations are available that supposedly taste awful enough to discourage cannibalism, but, in our experience, they don't work well.

As chicks grow, they may start picking at the base of the tail. Mature chickens often start picking near the vent. Sometimes, you can identify a ring leader or a single persistent picker, and removing that bird from the flock may resolve the problem.

An injury of any sort provides a terrific opportunity for picking to start. Whenever a bird has been injured in any way, move it into isolation until the wound has healed completely.

In grown chickens, boredom is less likely to occur when they spend time outdoors with adequate space to run around and to scratch and dust in, and where they can find all manner of things to peck at besides each other. Also, be sure all birds can easily get to feed and water stations. When cannibalism is just getting started, supplementing the flock's diet with alfalfa meal or sunflower seeds sometimes helps get the problem under control.

Eye guards that look like sunglasses–called blinders, peepers, or specs– are sometimes used to prevent cannibalism. They work by preventing a bird from seeing directly ahead to aim a peck. Their disadvantage, aside from making the chicken look embarrassingly ridiculous, is that the wearer may develop eye disorders.

Industrial chicken-raisers often deal with cannibalism by amputating the tips of the chickens' beaks, called debeaking or, euphemistically, beak trimming or beak conditioning. Debeaked chickens can't properly peck or groom themselves, and we think the deformity makes them look ugly. Anyone who loves their chickens wouldn't wish debeaking on them.

Once cannibalism has gotten started, it can be nearly impossible to stop unless the conditions that caused the problem in the first place are changed. Early prevention through vigilance, proper care, and rapid adjustments as needed are the best ways to deal with this perennial problem.

EGG-EATING

A particularly insidious form of cannibalism is egg-eating, which most chicken-keepers have to deal with at one time or another. You will know you have this problem when you find empty shells in the nest and yolk smeared around in the nesting litter or on other eggs. Egg-eating typically gets started when a hen accidentally breaks an egg in the nest, eats it, and finds out how good it is. Usually, an egg breaks because the shell is too thin, which may be a result of calcium deficiency.

Layer ration contains calcium, but usually not enough. If your hens have not had access to a calcium supplement in the form of crushed oyster shells, put out a supply. If they dive into it, calcium deficiency may well be the trouble. To make sure your hens get plenty of calcium, leave a containerful of oyster shells where they can get to it any time they feel the need.

Egg-eating may start when unground eggshells are fed back to the chickens. It's a great idea to recycle eggshells, but the shells should always be dried and mashed or ground in the blender. Feeding shells back to your hens does not provide an adequate amount of calcium, so it is not a complete substitute for oyster shell.

Boredom sometimes leads to egg-eating, so try to let the chickens out where they can scratch around and have plenty to do. Frequent collecting of eggs during the day removes temptation. Locating the nests in a darkened area usually helps discourage egg-eaters. Where moving a nest isn't practical, hang a fabric flap in the nest box opening to block direct light from shining into the nest.

If you can identify the guilty hen, isolate her for a while and hope she forgets about eating eggs. Roosters will also eat eggs, so the offender may not be a hen. To identify the culprit, look for the chicken literally with egg on its face.

Egg-eating can spread like wildfire through a flock, once others catch on to what they've been missing. If you see it starting, stop it while you can. We have occasionally had cases of egg-eating among our chickens, and all have been stopped by following the suggested procedures. But should you get an inveterate egg-eater, remove it permanently from the flock before it teaches its bad habit to the rest of the chickens, leaving you permanently eggless.

PARASITIC WORMS

Like young cats and dogs, young chickens have the tendency to pick up infestations of worms. The two main worm categories are familiar to dog and cat owners: roundworms (nematodes) and tapeworms (cestodes). However, the worm species that affect chickens are not the same as those that infect a dog or a cat, and therefore chickens cannot acquire worms from a dog or cat. Many of the worm species that affect chickens do affect other types of birds, including other poultry species as well as wild birds.

Some chicken-keepers deworm their chickens too often. Others don't deworm often enough. How often your chickens need deworming, or whether they need it at all, depends on numerous factors, such as your climate, how your flock is housed and managed, and the kind of worms that are present in your chickens' environment.

Chickens raised in a warm, dry climate are less at risk for a worm load than chickens raised in a damp climate. Chicken-keepers in dry climates sometimes claim their birds don't have worms because they're fed herbs or other natural concoctions. But the truth is that parasitic worm eggs and larvae in a dry environment quickly die when exposed to air and sunlight.

In a rainy climate, or in any area experiencing more than the usual amount of rainfall, worm eggs and larvae in the environment survive longer, because they are protected from drying out by moisture and mud. Since more parasites survive, the potential for a worm overload in chickens increases, and therefore more-aggressive parasite control and deworming measures are needed to avoid reduced resistance to disease.

Each worm species has one of two types of parasitic life cycles: direct or indirect. Direct-cycle worms move from one chicken to another by means of worm eggs or larvae expelled by an infected chicken into the environment that are then eaten by another chicken that thus becomes infected. Indirect-cycle worms must first enter some other creature during an immature stage of their lives. Such a creature–called an alternate or intermediate host–might be an ant, beetle, earthworm, fly, grasshopper, slug, snail, or termite. A chicken gets infected by eating the alternate host.

All tapeworms and more than half the roundworm species that infect chickens have indirect life cycles. Effective worm control therefore involves monitoring alternate hosts that can potentially infect your chickens. Beetles and grasshoppers, for instance, are more abundant in late summer. Earthworms come to the soil's surface after heavy rains. Slugs and snails are also more plentiful in warm, wet weather than in either cold weather or hot, dry weather.

The presence of alternate hosts is also influenced by flock housing and management. A caged chicken is most likely to be infected by flies. Chickens

🐔 DEWORMING

Of the many livestock dewormers on the market, the only one approved for chickens is piperazine, sold under the trade name Wazine, which is effective only against large roundworms, but not other roundworm species or tapeworms. Piperazine affects only adult worms, not the young worms attached to a chicken's intestinal lining. Treatment must therefore be repeated in 7 to 10 days to catch young worms that have matured and released their hold on the intestine. Piperazine is not approved for hens laying eggs for human consumption. The withdrawal period for meat birds is 14 days. The indiscriminate routine use of any dewormer is not the best answer to parasite control, because repeated use causes worms to eventually become resistant to the dewormer.

Despite convincing arguments to the contrary, do not rely on such things as garlic, pumpkin seeds, herbal concoctions, or diatomaceous earth as methods of deworming your chickens, especially if you would like to see them live long, healthy lives. Natural methods may control worms by making the environment inside a chicken less attractive to parasites, but unlike a chemical dewormer, they cannot be counted on to remove existing parasites.

The only way to know for certain if and when your chickens need deworming is through regular fecal tests. Most veterinarians offer fecal tests for a nominal fee and can tell you if your chickens are wormy, what kind of worms they have, how often they might require deworming, and what kind of dewormer to use. You can also learn to do your own fecal tests following directions available online. Luckily, once a healthy chicken reaches maturity, it becomes resistant to parasitic worms and is less in need of deworming.

housed on litter are most likely to be infected by cockroaches, beetles, and other indoor-living creatures. Free-range flocks are more likely to be infected by earthworms, grasshoppers, slugs, snails and other outdoor-living creatures. In a warm, humid climate, where alternate hosts are prevalent year-round, more aggressive deworming is required compared to a cold climate where alternate hosts are inactive for part of the year.

After a deworming treatment, thoroughly cleaning out and replacing coop litter reduces the rate of reinfestation. The spread of direct-cycle parasites may be minimized by having a droppings pit beneath the roost, so the chickens can't pick in the accumulating poop. Outdoors, rotating the run and either tilling the soil or mowing vegetation in the previous run reduces the parasite population by exposing expelled worms, larvae, and eggs to drying sunlight, helping reduce the overall population.

MITES AND LICE

Body parasites can be a serious problem for chickens. They crawl all over the head and body, biting and chewing and sucking blood until the poor bird is driven to distraction. These parasites can cause a good deal of blood loss, reducing the bird's resistance to disease. A setting hen provides an ideal stationary home for them, and they may so totally infest her body that she dies. Neither are mites and lice a pleasure to the person whose hand and arm are crawling with the things after handling an infested bird or equipment in the coop.

Chickens confined completely by a coop and run usually won't get mites or lice unless an affected chicken is brought in, and then the vermin will spread through the whole flock. When wild birds and rodents can gain access, they sometimes bring along body parasites and leave them with the flock.

All sorts of mites and lice can affect various parts of a chicken's body. Some kinds of mites spend the day on the perches and in the cracks of the coop but crawl onto the chickens at night, when they go to roost. Others live perpetually on the birds' bodies.

Mites are minute spiderlike specks that are difficult to see but may sometimes be observed by looking closely in the fluff between the feathers on the underside of a chicken, especially around the vent. They are red or light brown. If you see little bugs crawling around in the litter or nesting boxes, they are probably mites. The northern fowl mite is a particularly bad

Chicken louse

specimen because it spends its entire life cycle on a chicken's body, and each generation matures rapidly to produce another generation.

Lice are brownish yellow in color and are generally larger and thus easier to see than mites. They, too, spend their entire lives on the chicken's body. Their eggs, called nits, stick to the feathers in clumps and look something like gray rice. An easy way to reduce their population is to gather up and remove nit-laden feathers from the coop and yard during a molt.

If your chickens are exposed to lice and mites, check them occasionally

🐓 SCALY LEG MITES

Scaly leg mites may be spread by wild birds but are more often introduced by infected chickens. These pests, which are too tiny to see without a microscope, burrow under the scales on a chicken's shanks, generating debris that causes the scales to stick out and the shanks to appear rough and thickened. The irritation may cause the affected bird to do the goose step, like a Russian soldier, and eventually become lame.

These mites spread by traveling along the roost. They may be controlled by brushing the roost once a month with linseed oil or any kind of vegetable oil.

Getting rid of the mites on a chicken is not so easy, because they burrow in so deeply. Dipping each affected leg daily in vegetable oil is messy but works. Unless the infestation has been allowed to progress too far along, eventually the old scales will pop off and the shanks will become shiny and smooth. A less-messy method is to coat the shanks and feet with petroleum jelly, which stays on longer than drippy oil, so it needs to be applied only about once a week. Routinely applying oil or petroleum jelly to your chickens' shanks as part of your regular grooming routine will help prevent these mites from getting a foothold, or rather, a leghold, in the first place.

and eliminate the vermin before they get out of hand. Go out at night and examine one or two chickens. You won't have to check them all–if one has vermin, they all will. Avoid getting these parasites on your clothing and body. Should you fail, put the clothes in the washer and yourself in the shower.

Dust-bathing helps eliminate body parasites, so your chickens should be able to dust when they want to. If they don't have a natural dusting place, provide them with a bin of plain soft, dry dirt. The latest legally approved preparations designed to prevent or control body parasites are available at feed stores and from poultry-supply outlets. Treatment must be repeated, as directed on the label, to kill vermin that hatch after the first application.

TEN COMMON DISEASES OF BACKYARD CHICKENS

DISEASE	AFFECTS	CAUSE	TYPICAL SIGNS	PREVENTION
Avian pox	Skin	Virus	White bumps become scabs, then scars	Avoid contact with infected chickens; control mites, flies, mosquitoes
Bumblefoot	Foot pad	Bacteria	Abscess on bottom of foot; lameness	Soft bedding, low roosts
Coccidiosis	Intestines	Protozoa	Diarrhea, often bloody	Good sanitation; see page 91
Chronic respiratory disease	Respiration	Virus	Swollen face, coughing, sneezing, no odor	Avoid contact with infected chickens
External parasites	Skin and feathers	Mites and lice	Itching and feather damage	See page 129
Infectious bronchitis	Respiration	Virus	Coughing, sneezing, reduced laying, poor-quality eggs	Avoid contact with infected chickens
Infectious coryza	Respiration	Bacteria	Swollen face, labored breathing, foul odor	Avoid contact with infected chickens
Internal parasites	Intestines primarily	Worms	Paleness, weight loss or slow growth	See page 127
Marek's disease	Nerves	Virus	Transient paralysis	Vaccinate chicks or isolate them from mature chickens until 5 months old
Sour crop	Crop	Yeast	Oversize crop with sour odor	Good sanitation; avoid use of antibiotics

DIRE DISEASES

Even in the healthiest of chicken flocks, the occasional bird may die. So finding a dead chicken in your yard, as tragic as that may be, is no reason to become totally unglued. A rational approach would be to watch your remaining chickens for signs of disease. Of course, if more than one chicken suddenly die, you will certainly want to find out whether or not you have an epidemic on your hands and what you should do about it.

Disease organisms are always lurking about the coop, waiting for a chance to pounce on a likely victim. These organisms may be kept under control through periodic cleaning and disinfecting of the coop and related equipment. To ensure your chickens have healthy immune systems, provide adequate space, fresh air, and a nutritionally balanced diet.

By far the best way to introduce some dire disease into your backyard flock is to bring in new chickens. Much can be said for maintaining a closed flock–that is, one to which additions are not made through outside sources. Any time a new chicken is brought into your flock, it brings with it the possibility of potential problems. If you wish to expand your flock, the safest way is to acquire chicks and raise them yourself.

If you must bring mature birds into your flock, or when returning show birds home from a competition, isolate them for at least a month to see if any symptoms of disease develop. Doing so may be a nuisance but could prevent the loss of an entire flock that was formerly healthy.

Since a chicken may be a carrier of a disease for which it shows no signs, you may want to put a chicken (one that you are willing to sacrifice) into isolation with the new or returning birds. If your chicken does not develop any signs within about a month, then it, along with the new ones, may be returned to the flock.

Recognizing the signs of disease will help you provide prompt treatment. The best way to recognize signs of disease is to know what healthy chickens look and act like. Then you will readily notice when something is wrong with one or more of your birds.

Signs of illness in chickens are many and varied. Some signs are indicative of several different diseases, making diagnosis difficult even for an experienced veterinarian unless lab tests are performed. To make matters worse, a sick chicken will hide its misery as long as possible to avoid showing any sign of weakness to the bullies in the flock or to potential predators.

🐓 A WORD ABOUT BIRD FLU

Avian influenza, or bird flu, is a viral disease common in wild aquatic birds, which themselves rarely become ill but can spread the virus to other species. Just like the viruses for which we humans are offered flu shots every fall, bird flu viruses keep mutating and developing new strains. All the various bird flu viruses fall into one of two categories based on their pathogenicity—the degree to which they are capable of causing disease.

Low-pathogenic avian flu viruses are common throughout the United States, as well as in the rest of the world. They rarely cause disease in chickens but are of concern, because they can mutate into highly pathogenic viruses.

High-pathogenic avian flu viruses spread rapidly and produce serious, typically fatal, illness in chickens. And the disease is not always purely respiratory. The viruses may affect digestion (causing appetite loss and diarrhea), reproduction (reduced laying and soft-shelled eggs), or nerves (resulting in twisted necks and paralyzed wings). Sometimes, the first sign is the sudden death of healthy-looking chickens. To keep the disease from spreading, whenever a high-pathogenic virus is detected, the entire flock is destroyed.

How high-pathogenic flu gets around is a matter of contention. It may be introduced by migratory birds passing through an area where large numbers of industrial poultry reside. It is then spread by workers who travel from one industrial facility to another, causing outbreaks in completely confined industrial flocks. Indeed, studies show that avian influenza doesn't necessarily follow migratory flyways, but rather typically spreads along commercial trade routes. Bottom line: Even during one of the periodic outbreaks that flash through the poultry industry, the probability is low that your backyard chickens will become infected with bird flu.

Often, the first sign of illness in a hen is a decrease in egg-laying. But, of course, reduced egg production has many other causes, as described on page 51. Another sign of illness is sitting around listlessly with feathers ruffled. But if the weather is bad, ruffled feathers could simply mean the bird is cold. So watch for other signs: an unexplained drop in the amount of feed eaten, weight loss (a sharp, meatless breastbone can be the tip-off), wheezing and sneezing, runny nose, gulping, eyes swollen shut, yellow face and comb, black comb, lameness, and runny or bloody droppings (on the ground or sticking to feathers around the vent).

If you notice any of these signs in one of your birds, isolate it at once, well away from the others, to prevent spreading the disease and to allow the chicken to get plenty of rest. Chickens seem to know when one among them is weakened and will often pick on that one. Try to keep the ailing chicken warm, and especially avoid housing it in a drafty place. A light bulb placed nearby will provide warmth and might hasten recovery. Provide fresh feed and plenty of clean, fresh water. To avoid possibly spreading a disease, tend to your healthy chickens before caring for any in your ER. And carefully watch for further developments.

If several members of the flock appear affected, you would be wise to consult a vet or a veteran poultry-keeper in your area. Be selective in who you turn to for advice. Old-time folk remedies abound. Some may well be valid and effective treatments for chicken diseases; others may not do any good at all. Meanwhile, the ailing bird is suffering without proper help. Still other remedies may be downright detrimental and actually hasten the death of your favorite feathered friend.

Federal laws require a prescription before you can buy antibiotics or other medications to treat chickens. Find out in advance if a local vet is knowledgeable about poultry health and diseases. Getting professional help is especially prudent if a disease seems to be spreading among your flock. (For more information, *The Chicken Health Handbook,* by Gail Damerow, is a comprehensive source of chicken health-care information.)

We cannot overemphasize the fact that healthy chickens with strong immune systems, kept away from potential carriers of disease, fed properly, and housed in a clean, dry area of adequate size, are unlikely to come down with some dread disease.

STARTING YOUR FLOCK

The most difficult part of starting a flock of chickens is choosing a breed. The many available options can easily boggle your mind. This chapter brings together things to think about when you are ready to purchase your first chickens. In a way, it serves somewhat as a review of various considerations discussed elsewhere in this book. Here we will attempt to help you find answers to the most common questions asked by beginning chicken-keepers about starting a flock: "What kind of chickens do I want? How many shall I get? Should I start with eggs, chicks, or mature birds? Where should I get them? How do I avoid getting roosters? How much can I expect to pay?"

WHAT KIND OF CHICKENS?

When starting a new flock, the first decision is to determine your purpose in keeping chickens: to have fresh eggs, to raise fryers for the freezer, as fun pets, to compete at poultry shows, or any combination thereof.

Many breeds have been developed for a specific economic function. Generally, the heavy breeds were originally grown as meat birds, and their egg production is not all that great; the

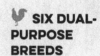

SIX DUAL-PURPOSE BREEDS

Delaware

Dominique

Iowa Blue

Plymouth Rock*

Rhode Island Red

Wyandotte

*Gail's top pick

lightweight breeds, on the other hand, are superior layers, but their slim, trim bodies make them a poor choice to raise as fryers.

For many backyard chicken-keepers, a good compromise for both eggs and meat is a so-called dual-purpose breed–not as efficient, and therefore not as economical, for producing either eggs or meat alone, compared to breeds intended specifically for one purpose or the other. For self-sufficiency, a dual-purpose breed is ideal, because you can hatch eggs from your own flock, keep the pullets as layers, and raise the cockerels for meat.

Hybrids are widely used for industrial egg or meat production, and are sold by most hatcheries that supply chickens for backyard flocks. The Rock Cornish cross is well-known for its excellent meat-producing qualities, while Leghorn crosses are among the top egg-layers. In many areas, sex links are

Comparison of sizes of large and bantam chickens

popular hybrids for backyard flocks. They are called sex links because the chicks' color is determined by genes on the sex chromosome, and their sex may be determined from the time they hatch by the color of their down.

The most common sex links are either red or black. Red sex links—sold under such trade names as Cinnamon Queen, Golden Comet, Gold Star, and Red Star—are slightly smaller and lay better than black sex links. Black sex links—sold under such trade names as Black Star, Black Rock, or Red Rock—lay larger eggs, are gentler in temperament, are quicker to mature, and, because they are somewhat larger, are considered to be more of a dual-purpose chicken. However, if your reason for a having a dual-purpose breed is for self-sufficiency, and you plan to hatch your own future chicks, hybrids are not the way to go.

One of the characteristics of a hybrid is its inability to replicate itself. Hybrids will reproduce—and vigorously—but the offspring will not be accurate reproductions of the parent stock. The nature of crossbreeds is to throw progeny with an unpredictable assortment of characteristics derived from the parent stock. Industrial poultry-keepers don't worry about this aspect, because they go back to the original cross to obtain eggs to hatch for replacements.

One year, we obtained some fantastic, huge, white chickens. The hens each laid a jumbo egg nearly every day. We collected some of the eggs to

hatch, so we could raise more of those wonder hens, but instead, we got a flock of chickens of the most varied assortment of sizes and colors. That's when we realized our whites were some type of crossbreed. To reproduce hybrids like these, you would have to find out how the original cross was made and acquire the breeding stock needed to do your own crossing. A simpler way of being certain you get exactly the hybrid strain you want is to buy that strain of chicks from a hatchery each time you need replacements.

Bantam breeds are about one-fourth to one-fifth the size of large breeds, generally weighing in the 2-pound range. They, therefore, eat correspondingly less and require less housing space. They lay smaller eggs, and fewer of them, and are typically kept as pets or for show. Bantam hens are valiant and tenacious setters, often employed as natural incubators by those who raise breeds that make less reliable mothers. Bantams are nice in the garden because they don't eat as much of the vegetation and don't scratch quite as destructively as the larger chickens. On the other hand, with the exception of Silkies, bantams can be more difficult to confine, because they fly more readily than most large breeds. And a high-pitched banty rooster's crow can be ear-piercing up close, while roosters of the larger breeds generally have a deeper, though louder, crow.

Personal preference plays a large role in choosing a breed. You might prefer fancy chickens with feathered topknots like frilly bonnets, feathered feet, beards and muffs, unusual combs, extra toes, laced or spangled plumage, and on and on. Hatchery catalogs and web pages are filled with pictures that give you an idea of what the different breeds look like. You'll be happiest with your new flock if you pick a breed you like to look at.

You don't have to select just one breed, either, especially if you don't intend to hatch your own chicks. A lot of backyard flocks these days consist of one hen each of several different breeds. They'll get along just fine, as long as you choose breeds that are compatible in size and temperament. Most hatcheries offer specials consisting of an assortment of all bantams, or all heavy breeds, or all fancy breeds, and so forth.

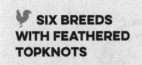 **SIX BREEDS WITH FEATHERED TOPKNOTS**

Crèvecoeur

Houdan

Polish*

Silkie

Sultan*

Spitzhauben

*Gail's top picks

Our first flock, already installed in the backyard of the house we moved into, looked like just such a hatchery special. No two chickens were alike. But a curious thing happened. The flock included roosters, some of the hens enjoyed raising chicks, and successive generations eventually began looking more like game chickens. In other words, genetically, the flock appeared to be reverting to the original jungle fowl type from whence all our modern breeds were derived.

STARTING FROM EGGS

Quite a few backyard flocks start out as a science project, so kids can watch eggs hatch. You might consider beginning your new flock with eggs, if you are able to obtain fertile eggs of the breed you choose, have access to an incubator, and are willing to try your luck with it. If you follow the manufacturer's instructions and don't have any accidents, about the best hatch rate you can expect is 85 percent. Let's say you use an incubator that holds seven eggs. You might hatch six chicks, you might hatch one, or you might hatch none. Many factors come into play–vitality of the parent stock, age of the eggs, how carefully the incubation instructions are followed, and so forth.

If you try to hatch eggs from a grocery store, the result will certainly be zero. Store-bought eggs are almost never fertile and have been refrigerated besides, so they surely won't hatch. Buy eggs that are sold specifically for hatching, which are called, fittingly enough, hatching eggs. Even though hatching eggs cost more than eating eggs, they come with no guarantee to hatch. Too many variables are not under the egg-seller's control. However, they should be guaranteed to be of the breed they were sold as, and to have been stored properly prior to the sale.

Another downside to starting with eggs, aside from the possibility that they might not hatch, is that approximately half of the chicks will be roosters. If you don't want roosters, or are not legally allowed to keep them, you'll need a plan for disposing of them. Even if you intend to include one or more roosters in your flock, you certainly don't want half of your chickens to be roosters.

Should you decide to start with hatching eggs, don't be afraid to be choosy. There is no point in wasting your time and money on eggs that might not hatch. When acquiring eggs through the mail, check out the seller to make sure previous customers were satisfied with the eggs and the way they were packed for shipment. If you buy your eggs in person, you will avoid the possibility that they will be unduly jostled or otherwise mishandled in transit. Scrambled eggs won't hatch. We knew one woman who would pick up her eggs one by one and shake them, saying, "I wonder if *this* one will hatch." Probably not.

STARTING WITH CHICKS

We highly recommend starting your first flock from chicks. Doing so gives you plenty of time to get acquainted with your chickens, and they with you, as you enjoy the experience of watching them grow and develop their individual personalities. You will avoid the frailties of incubating eggs, and you'll have the option of purchasing all pullets, should you so choose.

Most hatcheries and feed stores offer a choice of getting chicks either sexed or straight-run. Sexed chicks are sorted out as to whether they are pullets or cockerels. Straight-run chicks, also called as-hatched, are sold in the same proportion of pullets and cockerels as they came out of the eggs, usually 50-50, but too often 40-60 (60 percent cockerels). That works out fine, if you have a plan for the roosters, such as raising them as fryers. Sexed pullets are more expensive than straight-run, and, even so, some of them may turn out to be cockerels anyway.

All breeds are not available from sources that provide a sexing service, so you may have to settle for straight-run from the typical farmer, backyard hobbyist, or exhibition breeder. Chicks purchased from individuals will almost always be straight-run, because sexing is a specialized field requiring training and a good deal of practice. Please don't ask the person from whom you purchase chicks to trade pullets for your cockerels after the chicks have grown enough for you to tell the difference. Nearly everyone who raises chickens has

🐦 CHICK SEXING

Chicks may be sexed in one of the following five ways.

Vent sexing is a traditional Japanese method of examining minor differences in the tiny cloaca just inside a newly hatched chick's vent. Accuracy requires a great deal of training, skill, and keen observation. Even the most experienced vent sexers are only about 95 percent accurate.

Color sexing is done by examining the color and color patterns of a newly hatched chick's down. A few pure breeds may be naturally color sexed (called autosexing) by an experienced person, with about 85 percent accuracy. Color sexing of hybrids takes advantage of genetic combinations (called sex linkage) by which the down color of chicks differs between the females and the males. With minimal coaching, anyone can sort sex links with a high degree of accuracy.

Feather sexing is another sex-linked trait used for sexing hybrid chicks in which the newly hatched pullets have better developed wing feathers than the cockerels. This method works only if the chicks result from a cross between a hen of a slow-feathering breed and a cock of a rapid-feathering breed, yielding slow-feathering cockerels and rapid-feathering pullets. This method is not as accurate as color-sex linkage.

DNA testing is a process in which a specialized laboratory analyzes a chick's blood, down, or feathers, or the shell of the egg from which it hatched. This method is accurate, but expensive, and requires you to own the chick before you know its gender, or at least be willing to compensate the chick's seller.

Wait and see is the tried-and-true method of waiting until the chicks are several weeks along in development, during which the cockerels' combs and wattles become larger and brighter than the pullets, the cockerels of most breeds grow long, pointed hackle (neck) and saddle (lower back) feathers as well as more sweeping tail feathers, and, of course, the cockerels begin to crow.

the problem of too many roosters. Plan to deal with this issue on your own, either by buying sexed pullets, when possible, or by finding homes or recipes for your surplus cockerels.

The advantages of starting with chicks, rather than grown chickens, are that the chicks will learn to know you and more readily become pets; they are cheaper than mature birds; and they are less likely to carry diseases. There are disadvantages, too: Chicks require special facilities and care to get them through the critical growing stage, and some of them may die during the stress-filled maturation period. Moreover, when you buy chicks, you can't really tell what they will look like when grown. This consideration is especially important if you plan to show, because you'll want your new birds to closely conform to the *Standard*.

Instead of choosing between day-old chicks and mature chickens, a nice compromise is to get started chicks, if you can find them in the breed you want. Started chicks are partially grown, and the more growing stages they've passed through, the easier they will be for you to raise.

STARTING WITH GROWN CHICKENS

Starting a first flock with mature chickens puts you on the fast track toward egg production. However, you should know enough about your chosen breed to be able to tell a rooster from a hen. You should also be able to tell a young chicken from an old one, because a hen's egg-laying and cock's virility decline with age.

We've heard too many stories of people thinking that they got a real bargain on laying hens only to find that somebody peddled them worn-out hens from a commercial eggery. In fact, we know a young fellow who specializes in such sales. If you want so-called rescue chickens, fine, but at least you should be aware that's what you're buying.

A cock and a hen

One way to get an idea of a chicken's age is to look at its shanks: A young chicken will have smooth shanks, while an older bird's will be larger and slightly rougher. Check the breastbone, too, because a young chicken will have a flexible breastbone, while an older bird's breastbone will be more rigid. If a hen shows no characteristics of a layer (see Chapter 8), but indications are that she is no longer a pullet, don't let anyone con you with the line that she just hasn't started laying yet. It may well be true, of course, but, if so, it will be true forever.

Another pitfall of starting with grown chickens is that they are more likely than newly hatched chicks to have picked up a disease somewhere along their journey to chickenhood. Even if you choose to start your flock with grown chickens, do them and yourself a favor by not bringing more grown chickens into your flock later on. The result could be the heartsick experience of losing your original flock, your new chickens, or both. If you do decide to later add to your flock, bring home chicks and raise them yourself.

HOW MANY IS ENOUGH?

Chickens are social animals, so never get just one—it will get awfully lonesome. Two will keep each other company. Three is better. Should something happen to one, the remaining two will still have each other. On the other hand, just like people, chickens have favorite friends. With a flock of five, you'll likely find that three stick together, while the other two buddy up. Not that the two groups will fight. Rather, like humans, chickens enjoy spending more time in the company of their best friends.

After that, it's a matter of how many chickens you are legally allowed to keep, how much space you can provide, and why you want chickens. For eggs, consider that backyard hens average about one egg every 2 days and that three bantam eggs are roughly equivalent to two regular-size eggs. If you're raising chickens for meat, figure how many you can comfortably fit in your freezer, and add a few extra, in case you lose some.

And then, there's chicken math. One chicken leads to another. Pretty soon chicken-keeping becomes an obsession. There's always one more breed you want to try. Or a friend or neighbor offers to give you an extra chicken, or two, or three. Or a missing hen comes out from under the deck with a passel of peepers. Maybe someone gives you an incubator, and you want to see how it works. Or you stop at the farm store for a sack of feed, and on the way to check out, you pass a bin of adorable chicks for sale. How can you possibly resist? In preparation, you might consider starting small, expanding slowly, and plan in advance where you will stop.

SOURCING YOUR STARTER FLOCK

Let's start with where *not* to acquire your founding flock. Do not buy chicks, chickens, or hatching eggs from the following places: auctions, flea markets, swap meets, chicken shows, Craigslist, and chicken mills (the poultry equivalent of puppy mills). Doing so is taking a huge gamble on the possibility of battling a disease from the outset or buying misrepresented stock (age or breed).

The best place to acquire founding stock depends on what you want. Possibilities include the following:

Local feed store. In early spring, many feed stores offer chicks for sale. They may be sex-linked hybrids or a limited selection of purebreds. In some stores, the bins of chicks are labeled as to breed. In other stores, not even the employees can tell you which breeds are being offered. These chicks are generally inexpensive, because the store purchases them in large quantities and, further, expects to sell you feed and all manner of chick-raising gear.

Hatchery. Nearly every state has at least one hatchery that may specialize in certain breeds or hybrids or may offer a large variety of breeds. Even if you don't live near a hatchery, you can find the major hatcheries online that will ship chicks or eggs to you through the mail. Some hatcheries offer exhibition breeds, but only a few breed prizewinners. A bona fide hatchery maintains, or contracts with, poultry-breeding farms. Be aware that some online purveyors are not hatcheries, but brokers that obtain the stock they sell from one or more hatcheries and, therefore, have little or no control over the quality of the eggs or birds that they sell.

4-H Chick Chain. In some states, local 4-H clubs engage in Chick Chain projects, wherein participants receive baby chicks in the spring and sell laying-age pullets in the fall. This program, which started in Georgia in the mid-1900s, originally focused on production breeds but, in some areas, now encompasses fancy show breeds. Your county Extension agent will know if this program is active in your area.

Serious breeder. If you want quality purebred stock for exhibition purposes, look for a serious breeder who keeps records on breeding, production,

🐓 MAIL-ORDER CHICKS

Chicks shipped by mail can survive for as long as 3 days without eating and drinking. During incubation, the developing embryo draws nutrients from the egg's yolk. By the time the bird hatches, not all of the yolk has been used up. What remains is drawn into the chick's abdomen and absorbed by the chick's body during its first 3 days of life.

Nature provides these reserve nutrients, because eggs incubated under a hen don't all hatch at the same time. The early-hatchers therefore have sufficient reserves to hang around under the hen waiting for the stragglers to catch up. Even when all the eggs hatch at nearly the same time, the extra yolk reserves give hatchlings plenty of time to learn what to eat and drink, and where to find it.

The incubation of chicks destined to be shipped by mail is scheduled so they all hatch at once. They, therefore, all have the same amount of yolk reserves and may be shipped together, giving them up to 3 days before they need to start drinking and eating. To facilitate timely delivery, mail-order shipments are generally scheduled to go out early in the week, so the chicks don't end up spending a weekend languishing at a postal facility.

and growth. If possible, make a personal visit so you can ask questions, examine records, and see the conditions under which the birds live. To find well-known breeders of the breed you are interested in, attend poultry shows to see who typically produces the top prizewinners, and join the appropriate breed club, which more than likely will publish a directory of members. The newspaper *Poultry Press* (or Canada's *Feather Fancier*) offers monthly commentary on who's winning at shows and who has birds for sale.

If you're looking for a heritage breed, the Livestock Conservancy or Rare Breeds Canada can help you find a producer. Seek one who specializes in the specific chickens you want, has worked with the same flock for a long time, and has taken the trouble to trace the flock's history to verify that it is an original strain. Unless the breed you are interested in is autosexing, chicks purchased from a private breeder are likely to be sold straight-run.

COST FACTORS

Several factors determine the initial cost of a chicken. The price you pay will depend a lot on the breed you buy. Some breeds are harder to find, tricky to raise, or in greater demand, and therefore will be more expensive. The closer to maturity a bird is, the more investment the breeder has in it, in time as well as money, so the more the bird will likely cost.

Season may also have some bearing on prices. Grown chickens bought in the spring will often be more expensive than those purchased in autumn, because the breeder has fed them through the unproductive winter season. Breeders like to reduce their flocks in the fall, which is often bargain time for buyers who don't mind winter feeding. For this same reason, laying hens will be more difficult to find in the spring. People often don't want to purchase hens until the laying season starts, and competition for those available in spring is much greater. Fine show birds are priced by appearance more than by season: The closer the bird conforms to the *American Standard of Perfection*, the higher the asking price.

We would like to quote specific prices to give you an idea of what to expect, but doing so is entirely impractical because prices vary widely with such things as the locale, the season, the breed, the age, and fluctuations in the cost of feed. The best way to get an idea of what to expect to pay is to check several sources and compare their prices. A good place to start is with online hatcheries, some of which sell feathered chickens as well as newly hatched chicks. When comparing online prices to local prices, don't forget to factor in the cost of shipping.

Occasionally, you will find chickens going for substantially less than the prevailing rates. Emergency liquidations of flocks may be required, for example–estate settlements ("He left us his *what*?"), divorce cases ("Who gets custody of the chickens?"), and unanticipated landscaping alterations ("They ate my pelargoniums!"). If you keep an eye out for the breed you want and are willing to wait, you may find it for almost any price, maybe even for free. But be on the alert, especially when a supposed bargain is in the offing. Following the used-car buyers' philosophy, try to bring along a friend who knows chickens to help confirm your judgment.

CHICKENS FOR FUN

We don't have a television. We don't need one. Our desire for passive entertainment is satisfied by a show that doesn't use electricity. Best of all, it's never interrupted by commercials. We simply climb into our cherry tree armchair and instantly become absorbed in the intrigues of barnyard society. There's only one channel, it's true, but the programming is live, in color, and endlessly varied: We can referee crowing contests, watch a hen proudly parade her newly hatched chicks around, or cheer for the little guy in a soccer game involving a freshly found worm. It's a marvelous excuse to put off mowing the lawn or doing the dishes. Sometimes, we run out to get eggs for breakfast and don't get back till lunchtime.

Spending time with the flock and getting to know each chicken is made all the more charming by the fact that each has its own personality. Some are aggressive, having an opinion on every subject; others are unassuming, the type you hardly notice; one now and then is inquisitive, quite oblivious to the hazards of hanging around the business end of an operating garden tool; some talk all the time, muttering away to no one in particular the whole day long as they make their rounds, and no one in particular paying them a bit of attention. The roosters' crows are distinctive enough that the owner can easily identify each bird—even from under the covers at

SIX FRIENDLY BANTAM BREEDS

Belgian Bearded d'Anvers

Belgian Bearded d'Uccle*

Booted Bantam

Nankin

Pyncheon

Silkie*

*Gail's top picks

SIX FRIENDLY LARGE BREEDS

Cochin*

Faverolle

Langshan

Sultan

Sussex

Yokohama

*Gail's top pick

the break of dawn. People who don't raise chickens are amazed when the owner of a flock can point out each chicken by name and mention some distinguishing characteristic by which the bird may be uniquely identified. To the uninitiated, they're all alike.

Observing the fantastic variety of subtle social interactions among chickens has given us insight into birds, in general. We find that many of the social customs of chickens apply to wild birds as well. Now when we see birds courting on the front lawn, their peculiar antics are not so mysterious to us.

Your friends may think you're crazy if you try to tell them how fascinating chickens are. But once they find out, they'll likely be hooked, too. It might even do something dramatic to them. We have a young friend who got a job helping an elderly man care for his flock. The fellow found the experience so compelling that he changed his college major to avian science.

The more time you spend with your chickens, the more quickly they will become pets. Chickens, like other pets, can become quite fond of their owners. They come when you call them, follow you around, and sit by you when you're pursuing outdoor activities, such as reading in the sunshine or working in the garden.

We can think of plenty of good reasons to raise chickens—for companionship, fresh eggs, delicious meat, bug and weed control, a continuous supply of fertilizer for the garden, prizes at the fair—but you really don't need a reason. Raising chickens is just plain fun!

APPENDIX: FURTHER INFORMATION

American Standard of Perfection, American Poultry Association (APA), amerpoultryassn.com. This volume lists the standards by which each recognized breed and variety is judged at exhibition, and it includes artwork of most breeds.

Bantam Standard, American Bantam Association (ABA), bantamclub.com. This book is similar to the APA *Standard* but deals with bantam breeds and varieties only.

The Chicken Chick, Kathy Shea Mormino, the-chicken-chick.com. This website analyzes the latest trends in chicken-keeping and separates fact from fiction.

The Chicken Encyclopedia, Gail Damerow, storey.com/books/the-chicken -encyclopedia. From addled to wind egg, this volume demystifies terminology peculiar to American chicken-keepers.

The Chicken Health Handbook, Gail Damerow, storey.com/books/the-chicken -health-handbook-2nd-edition. This comprehensive guide explains how to maximize your flock's wellness and deal with health issues.

Feather Fancier, Ontario, Canada. This monthly Canadian newspaper is similar to the US's *Poultry Press.*

Hatching and Brooding Your Own Chicks, Gail Damerow, storey.com/books /hatching-brooding-your-own-chicks. A comprehensive guide detailing everything you need to know about incubating eggs and raising baby chicks.

The Livestock Conservancy, livestockconservancy.org. This US organization works to protect heritage breeds of poultry and other livestock from the danger of extinction.

Poultry Press, poultrypress.com. This monthly US newspaper is a major source of information on poultry exhibitions, organizations, breeds, and breeding.

Rare Breeds Canada, rarebreedscanada.org. Canada's equivalent to the Livestock Conservancy in the United States.

Showing Poultry, Glenn Drowns, storey.com/books/showing-poultry. This book, written by a poultry judge, offers guidance on successfully exhibiting your poultry at fairs and expositions.

Storey's Guide to Raising Chickens, Gail Damerow, storey.com/books/storeys-guide
-raising-chickens-4th-edition/. A complete guide to chicken-keeping, feeding, care,
and facilities.

Storey's Illustrated Guide to Poultry Breeds, Carol Ekarius, storey.com/books
/storeys-illustrated-guide-to-poultry-breeds/. This book includes much
the same information as the APA *Standard* but is considerably more entertaining,
and it includes photographs.

INDEX

breeds of chickens (*cont.*)
  hybrids (hybrid-crosses/crossbreeds), 136–138, 141. *See also* Cornish chickens
  large breeds, 148
  for laying, 49
  meaty, 97
  noisy, 46
  purebreds, 2, 97, 100–101, 144–145
  rare, 73
  sexing and, 141
  temperament of, 139
bronchitis, 131
brooders
  brooding meat birds, 97–98
  defined, 6
  dust from, 86–87
  heat source for, 86
  litter/bedding for, 6, 87, 91
  locating, 86–87
  setting up, 85–87
  temperature for, 87–88
brooding. *See* setting hens
bumblefoot, 131
butchering chickens. *See* meat, chickens for

calcium
  deficiency of, 55, 126
  in eggshells, recycling, 33–34
  starter rations and, 71
  supplemental, 51, 126
Campine chickens, 49, 111
candling eggs, 5, 79–81
cannibalism, 6, 124–126. *See also* egg-eating
carrying chickens, 117
catching chickens, 116–117
chicken tractors, 20, 21, 68
chickens
  basic information and definitions, 1–7
  for fun, 147–148

gender names defined, 1
  as house pets, 93
  names for, defined, 1–3
  types of, defined, 1–3
  words to know, 1–7
chicks
  communicating with mother hen, 68
  cost factors for buying, 145–146
  foster mothers for, 69–71
  growing up, 91–92
  hens setting to hatch. *See* setting hens
  incubating eggs for. *See* incubators
  isolating hens and, 71–72
  mother hen caring for, 71–72
  sources of, 144–145
  spring hatching, 61–62
  starting flocks with, 140–142
  vigor of, hatching time and, 62
chicks, caring for, 85–92. *See also* brooders
  about: overview of, 85
  feeding chicks, 89–91
  growth process and, 91–92
  integrating flocks, 93–94
  pasting up (pasty butt, sticky bottom) and, 90
  pecking-order squabbles, 92–93
  starter rations, 30, 36, 71, 87, 90, 91
  treats and, 91
  water for chicks, 88–89
chronic respiratory disease, 131
classifications of pure breeds, 2
cleaning coops, 26
clipping wings, 117–118
cluckers, 69. *See also* setting hens
clutch, defined, 5
coccidiosis (coccy), 6, 90–91, 99, 131
coccidiostat, 6
Cochin chickens, 16, 18, 65, 88, 109, 110, 111, 148
cock fights, 46

dual-purpose breeds, 135
dust, brooders and, 86–87
dust baths, 6–7, 15, 16, 37, 131

egg-eating, 6, 33, 52, 126–127
eggs, 49–59. *See also* fertility of eggs;
    hatching; setting hens
  age of chickens laying, 49
  autumn molt and, 51
  binding in oviduct, 54–55
  bloom/cuticle on, 5, 56–57
  boosting winter laying, 52
  calcium in shells recycled, 33–34
  cleanliness of, 56–57, 74
  clutch, defined, 5
  collecting, 52–53
  colors of, 54, 55
  fake, types and function, 52–53
  fluctuations in laying, 51–52
  freezing, 58–59
  helping hens lay, 54–55
  hidden by layer, 53
  laying time table, 52
  longevity of layers, 50–52
  nesting boxes and, 25–27
  production process, 52
  pullets starting to lay, 49–50
  reduced laying of, 51
  refrigerating, 57
  rotting, 80
  separating breeds before hatching, 62
  sexing myth, 63
  sizes of, 55
  starting flocks with, 139–140
  storing, 57–59
  top breeds for laying, 49
electricity, in coops, 28

Faverolle chickens, 88, 111, 148
Fayoumi chickens, 19, 49, 120
Feather Fancier newspaper, 108, 145

feathered topknots, breeds with, 138
feather-legged breeds, 88
featherless brood patch, 61
feathers
  missing, losing, 45, 123–124
  plucking, 100, 102–103
  wing-clipping, 117–118
feeders, 36–37
feeding chickens, 30–45
  amount of feed, 31, 32
  cannibalism and, 6, 124–126
  changing feed gradually, 36
  chick care, 89–91
  crumbles and, 31, 90
  egg-eating and, 126–127
  feeders for, 36–37
  free-range foraging, 33–34
  grit and, 3, 32–34
  growing feed and, 35
  meat birds, 98–100
  mixing your own rations, 35–36
  pellets, 31
  prepared feeds, 30–31
  scratch and, 3, 32, 69
  starter rations and, 30, 36, 71, 87,
    90, 91
  storing feed, 27, 36
  treats, 32, 91
  watering and, 38–40, 88–89, 98,
    120–121
  when to feed, 31
female chickens, terms for, 1
fence, building, 14–17
fertility of eggs. *See also* setting hens
  assessing, 56, 79–80
  candling and, 79–81
  defined, 4
  dormancy and, 62–63
  factors affecting, 4
  internal blood spots and, 5, 56
  number of roosters and, 44–46
  nutritive value of eggs and, 56
  pullets starting to lay and, 49–50

Orpington chickens, 15, 55, 65, 100, 111, 122
oviduct, 3, 54

parasites
    mites and lice, 129–131
    worms, 127–129
pasting up (pasty butt, sticky bottom), 90
pecking order, 7, 46, 92–93
pellets, 31
Penedesenca chickens, 34
perches
    chicks starting to use, 92
    defined, 1
    roosting bars, 21–23
    swinging, 22
perching, 1, 92
pets, chickens as, 4, 93, 138, 141, 148
physiology of chickens, terms related to, 3
pips and pipping, 5, 82, 97
plucking chickens, 100, 102–103
Plymouth Rock chickens, 15, 96, 97, 100, 109, 111, 135
Polish chickens, 66, 111, 120, 138
poop. See droppings
Poultry Press newspaper, 108, 145
predators. See protecting chickens
premiums and premium list, 110–112
protecting chickens, 8–11
    about: overview of, 8
    building fence for, 14–17
    catching marauders, 118–119
    dogs and, 9–10, 119–120
    isolating hens/chicks and, 71–72
    kids and, 10–11
    from predators, 118–120
    roosters as protectors, 43–44
    stories you want to avoid, 8–9
    treading and, 45

pullets
    butchering, 100
    chick selection and, 140–141
    defined, 1
    egg size, 55
    layer longevity and, 50–51
    laying eggs. See eggs
    pecking order and, 92–93
    sexing, 5, 63, 141
    showing. See showing chickens
purebreds, 2, 97, 100–101, 144–145

quantity of roosters/chickens, 44–45, 143–144

raising chickens. See also specific topics
    reasons for, xi–xii
    saving money, xi
    starting point, xi. See also flock, starting
    this book and, xi–xiii
    words to know, 1–7
rare breeds, 73
Redcap chickens, 73, 111
refrigerating eggs, 57. See also freezing eggs
resources, additional, 149–150
respiratory disease, chronic, 131
Rhode Island Red chickens, 2, 46, 49, 100, 110, 111, 135
Rhode Island White chickens, 55, 111
rodents, controlling, 37, 120
roost, defined, 1
roosters, 41–48
    cock definitions and, 1, 41
    crowing, 47–48
    dancing, 43
    defined, 1
    fighting (cock fights), 46
    hens and, 41, 42–43, 44–46
    mating ratios (to hens), 44

Printed in the United States
by Baker & Taylor Publisher Services